Revisions of Space

Revisions of Space

An Architectural Manual

Dick van Gameren

with an afterword by
Hans Ibelings

NAi Publishers

Acknowledgements

Compilation and text: Dick van Gameren
Afterword and editing: Hans Ibelings
Copy editing: D'Laine Camp
Translation: Peter Mason
Picture editing: Dick van Gameren, Sebastiaan Kaal
Analytical drawings: Sebastiaan Kaal
Design: Studio LSD with Dominic Saves and Luis Castañeda, Rotterdam
Printing: Drukkerij Die Keure, Bruges
Paper: IJsselprint 140 g/m², Hello gloss 135 g/m²
Project coordination: Anneloes van der Leun, NAi Uitgevers
Publisher: Simon Franke, NAi Uitgevers

With thanks to Max Risselada, all colleagues and staff of de architectengroep, the clients and consultants of our projects, Paul Meurs, Paolo Zimbres.

NAi Publishers is an internationally orientated publisher specialized in developing, producing and distributing books on architecture, visual arts and related disciplines.
www.naipublishers.nl info@naipublishers.nl

It was not possible to find all the copyright holders of the illustrations used. Interested parties are requested to contact NAi Publishers, Mauritsweg 23, 3012 JR Rotterdam, The Netherlands.

Available in North, South and Central America through D.A.P./Distributed Art Publishers Inc, 155 Sixth Avenue 2nd Floor, New York, NY 10013-1507, Tel 212 6271999, Fax 212 6279484.

Available in the United Kingdom and Ireland through Art Data, 12 Bell Industrial Estate, 50 Cunnington Street, London W4 5HB, Tel 208 7471061, Fax 208 7422319.

Printed and bound in Belgium

ISBN 90-5662-443-1

Contents

Introduction

The current debate on architecture pays excessive attention to visual appearance. This is as true of conceptual architecture, in which a building is reduced to an emblematic illustration of an idea, as it is of architecture that is often viewed as the opposite of this conceptualism, namely the traditionalist architecture that derives its significance mainly from the familiarity of the historicizing images used. However beautiful the results may sometimes be, both extremes usually yield an impoverished architecture that is caught in the grip of either an obsessive striving for conceptual originality or a slavish copying of historical examples.

This obsession with visual effect can also be found in the many design assignments that are little more than the demand for an image. Aspects relating to programme and space are predetermined in standard solutions tailored to suit the demands of the market. The focus on the image may satisfy the current demand for diversity and identity, but fails to reconcile that demand for identity and diversity with the simultaneously growing demand for densification and concentration. This question arises in connection with every intervention in the existing city, but also in the development of new suburban areas.

In the present period of globalisation, direct confrontations between different cultures and the growth of individualisation, the definitions of identity and diversity, collective and community are not without ambiguity. That is why it is necessary to redefine terms like private, collective and public, as well as their relation to one another. This calls for new architectural models in which pride of place is given to the relation between space and function. The tendency to ignore that relation and to fall back on familiar images does not solve anything. On the contrary, it exacerbates potential conflicts.

The quality and feasibility of a plan are determined not by appearance, but by the way in which it sets spatial connections and movements in motion. The creation of spatial links and the design of movement through the space are the distinctive aspects of architecture. Architects often tend to talk or write about nothing but that which is related to architecture, while rarely talking or writing about architecture itself. The present book is an exception: it describes architecture as a system of spaces and movements.

The book is based on a selection from my own work and examples from the past that raise the question of spatial connections and movements. Although the link between history and contemporary design is evident to me, it is not a common combination. It was found in the 1950s in the *Architectural Review*, in which architects such as Gordon Cullen and architectural historians like Nikolaus Pevsner combined contemporary architecture, history, analysis and criticism, but it is impossible to find this combination today; everyone seems to be forced to retreat into his own niche. Design and history are separate worlds, and the historians and the designers have developed essentially different attitudes towards the past, as Hans Ibelings describes in his afterword. For architects, that relation disappointingly often consists of a denial or ignorance of what has been achieved in the past.

By advancing a series of historical examples, I would like to argue a second case: the case for an intelligent use of history. The historical examples in this book are projects that have inspired me, and that have brought home to me the importance of spatial links and movements. This book is not a comprehensive historical survey, and it is certainly not an objective history of architecture either. It is a plea for a critical reappraisal of designs from the past, in which history is not a catalogue of styles that can be duplicated, but a practical inspiration for new solutions and a catalyst to escape from the current stagnation in architectural debate and practice.

Dick van Gameren

I Space in Buildings

R R

R R

The first sentence of Nikolaus Pevsner's introduction to *An Outline of European Architecture* (1943) is famous but no longer true: 'A bicycle shed is a building; Lincoln Cathedral is a piece of architecture.' The distinction between a building and a piece of architecture is not a relevant theme any longer, since everything can be architecture.

If a piece of architecture and a building are treated as synonyms, the second sentence of Pevsner's introduction, which is very rarely cited, becomes much more interesting: 'Nearly everything that encloses space on a scale sufficient for a human being to move in is a building.' Space alone is not a sufficient criterion of architecture; it has to be space in which people can move.

The relation between space and movement in architecture, like that between mass and space, is not a relation between opposites, but a complementary one, even though Adolf Loos claimed that the origin of architecture is the creation of space, which led him to criticise architects who, in his view, only created mass. (However, Loos was right when he said that more attention is usually paid in architecture to the form of the mass than to the form of the space.) Mass enables space, and space enables movement.

It may be a commonplace that architecture arises from an interaction between mass, space and movement, but the design of the movement seems to play a minimal role in many designs, resulting in buildings that are little more than a sculpture or a three-dimensional functional arrangement.

The history of architecture is not usually considered from this perspective either; the form of the mass dominates the form of the space there, too. Taking a serious look at movement through space, however, affords insight into buildings that are otherwise valued for other reasons or ignored. Moreover, it offers ways of approaching the design of movement through space, one of the most important and distinctive aspects of architecture.

A genre of buildings that is usually only dealt with in passing, if at all, in architectural history is the medieval castle. The theme of movement through the space often plays a major role in castles. It is precisely the combination of the contradictory demands of defensibility, achieved by a maximum of mass, and inhabitability, which requires space, that results in an interesting tension, and one that has been resolved in ingenious ways. An example is the twelfth-century keep of **Dover Castle**. The two rectangular main living areas are enclosed by a hollow wall six to eight metres thick. The cavity accommodates two spiral staircases and a number of separate secondary areas which can be reached from the two main ones.

The combination of mass and space can also be found in the main keep of the fourteenth-century Dutch castle **De Doornenburg** near Bemmel. The ground plan of the keep is extremely simple, but the ingenious spatial organisation is manifested in the cross-section. The castle contains two interconnected spatial systems. One of them consists of a series of rooms that wind their way upwards in a spiral, appearing as a split level in cross-section. At right angles to them, a straight flight of stairs runs through the thick intermediate wall and provides access to each of the rooms separately.

The spatial complexity of castles arises from their complex use. They accommodated people from all walks of life. Separate circuits were therefore often created and rooms with limited access were isolated from the rest to avoid undesirable confrontations between the classes. Placing circulation and smaller rooms in the wall leads to a reversal: the living spaces are static, while the mass that brings about the connections and facilitates those movements through the building is dynamic. In such a case, it is the mass and not the living space that determine the spatiality.

Robert Smythson and his sons, a family of English architects active around 1600, have left a number of buildings and designs in which the space for circulation is at first hollowed out in the mass, then expands, and eventually comes to occupy an increasing amount of the total space.

The circuit eventually came to structure the entire design, subordinating practically all the rooms to the circulation. A number of the houses that they designed in a river valley near Chesterfield demonstrate this development.

In **Barlborough Hall** (1583–1585) the space is organised horizontally. The house has two circuits: a 'genuine' circuit at the centre around a light shaft, and a second circuit in the form of a linking of all the rooms at the level of the façade. The vertical link is incorporated entirely in the walls: a spiral staircase, illuminated from above by a lantern.

The inner walls separating the rooms are very thick and contain niches and hearths; the openings leading from one room to another are cabinet-like passages. The outer wall, on the other hand, is very thin and fitted with enormous windows. The architect thus reversed the traditional construction of a heavy outer wall and light inner walls.

In 1587 Robert Smythson commenced work on **Hardwick Hall**, which radically continues the same theme by providing spatial continuity not only horizontally but also vertically. In this immense house, the vertical link is also liberated from the mass to form a route that winds through the entire building. This route, in essence a continuous stairway, is particularly impressive for the effect of spatial culmination. The route passes through the storeys, growing higher and lighter from floor to floor, to culminate in the long gallery: a vast hall fifty metres long and almost eight metres high. At the other end of this long gallery, the route continues downwards until, after many changes of direction, it eventually re-enters the central hall. More than one historian has characterised Hardwick Hall as a precursor of twentieth-century Modernist architecture because of the complex route and the enormous glass surfaces. In fact, Nikolaus Pevsner found the continuous stairway so unusual that he doubted its authenticity as a sixteenth-century invention. The capricious movement through the house is a pragmatic solution to prevent the stairway from ending directly in the long gallery that extends the entire length of the building, which would have been the case if the stairway had been a conventional one that linked the floors directly above one another.

One important result of this stairway is that all the main rooms in the building are directly accessible via the various landings without the need for other passages. Besides, the stairway clearly distinguishes the more public areas from the private ones. The stairway provides access to the public rooms in the house: the hall on the ground floor, the chapel on the first floor, and the reception rooms on the top floor. Access to the private rooms is via the landings, like modern apartments which are accessible from a gallery. The complex spatiality is accompanied by a strict functional organisation and a separation of public and private areas.

The ideas and principles developed in Hardwick Hall lapsed into oblivion during the period in which formal and classical views dominated architecture. Only three centuries later, once again in England, with the Arts and Crafts Movement a new interest arose in a spatiality that did not consist of a symmetrical disposition of rooms, but was based on movement through the building. That is why the Arts and Crafts Movement is often viewed as a precursor of Modernism, motivated by the desire on the part of modern architects and historians to claim dynamic spatiality as a typically modern property.

The ground plan of the Arts and Crafts house is centred on the hall, which is no longer just the public reception room of the country house, but also an important part of the private rooms.

The architect M.H. Baillie Scott ingeniously used stairways and passages to connect the hall with the adjacent rooms in **Blackwell** House (1897–1900) beside Lake Windermere in the Lake District. The hall consists of a central, high part and several lower parts. It is immediately adjacent to two living rooms with hearths and bays with benches. The main stairway is situated in the high part of the hall and leads up to a passage overlooking the hall. A side staircase leads to a chamber above the hearth, which also overlooks the hall. The rooms and the circuit have been united by linking every room visually with the hall.

The small house that American architect Robert Venturi built for his mother in

Dover Castle, Dover Kent, UK
12th century

1

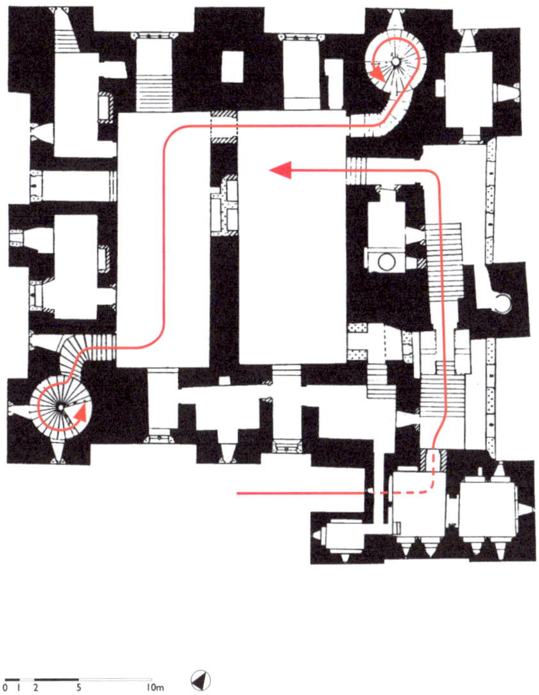

2

1 first floor of the keep
2 aerial view of the castle, with the keep in the middle

5

De Doornenburg, Doornenburg, NL

14th century

3

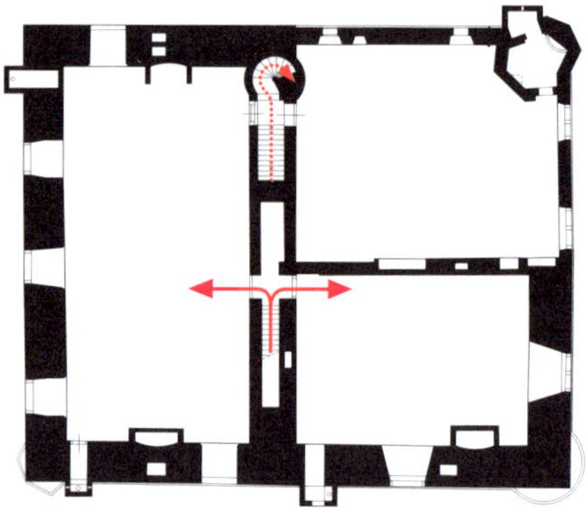

4

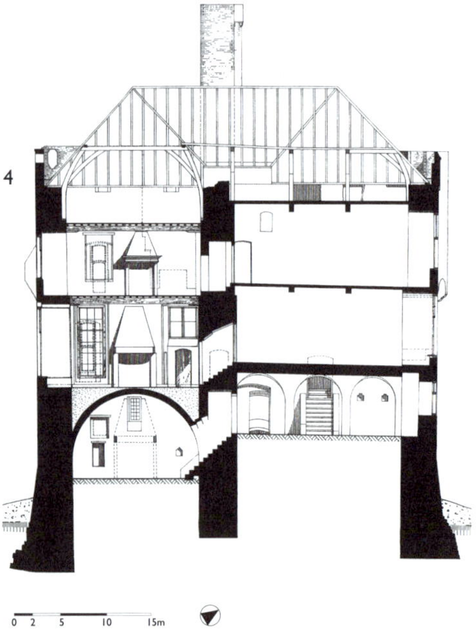

2

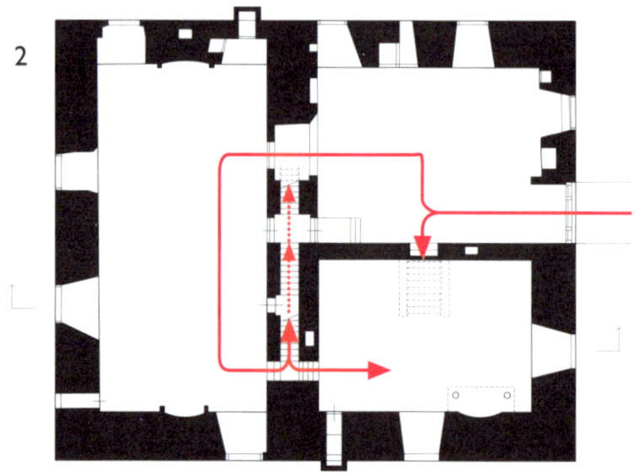

1

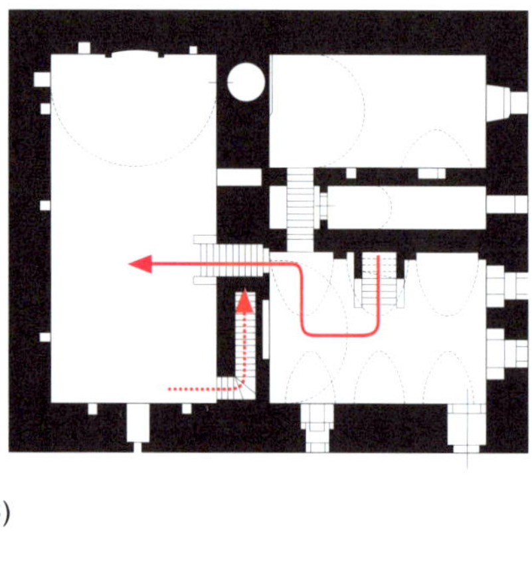

1 basement level (author's reconstruction)
2 ground floor
3 first floor
4 cross-section of transverse wall (measurements 1903)
5 castle seen from the southwest ca. 1910

Barlborough Hall, Derbyshire, UK
Robert Smythson
1583–1585

2

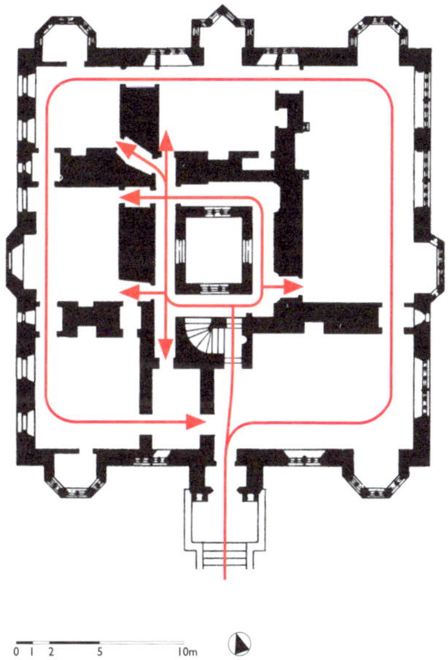

1

1 ground floor
2 front elevation

Hardwick Hall, Derbyshire, UK

Robert Smythson

1587–1599

3

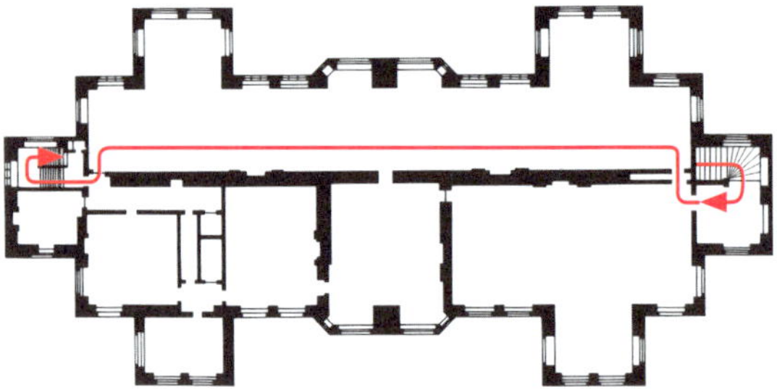

2

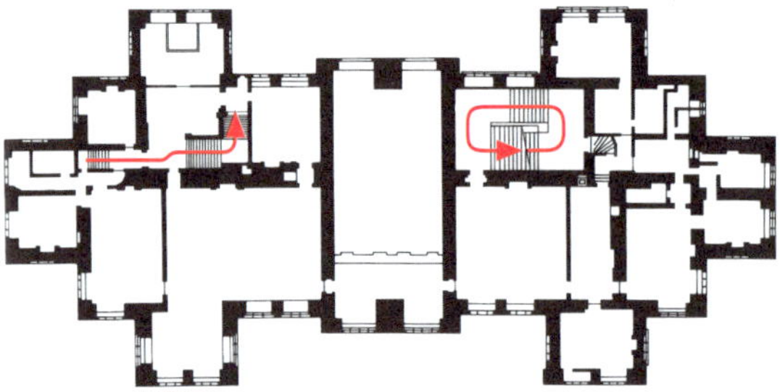

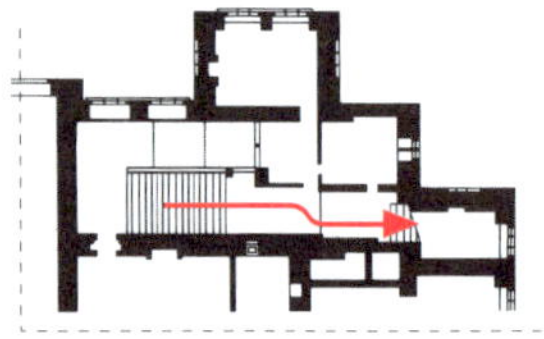

1

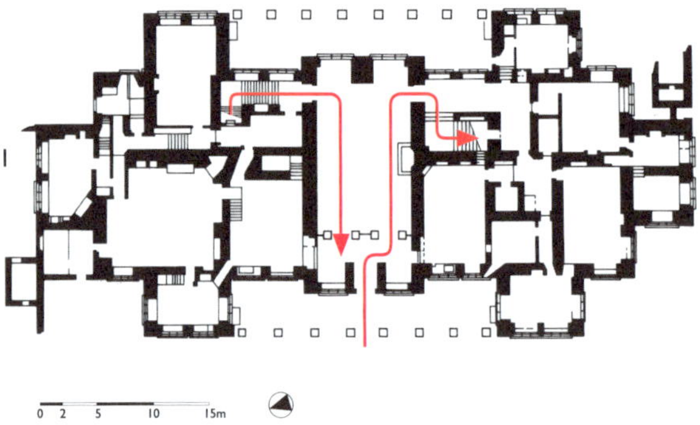

4

6

7

8

5

I ground floor
2 first floor and part of mezzanine
3 second floor
4 front elevation on entrance side
5 staircase between ground floor and first floor
6 landing between ground floor and first floor
7 staircase reaches second floor
8 stairs near chapel gallery, first floor

Blackwell, Bowness-on-Windermere, Cumbria, UK

Mackay Hugh Baillie Scott

1897–1900

2

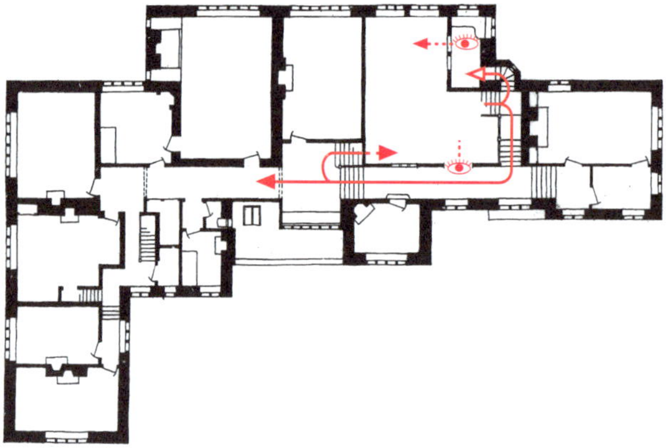

3

1

1 ground floor
2 first floor
3 hall with cabinet above hearth
4 hall
5 first floor corridor with view of hall on the right

4

5

Chestnut Hill, Pennsylvania (1961) is a surprising combination of the characteristics of the English country house. **Vanna Venturi House** has a hall with a hearth and a large staircase on the smallest possible surface area. On the first floor this links up with a second staircase that does not lead anywhere, but does effectively suggest space. The combination of the staircase and hearth results in an object that introduces a strong, expansive spatiality in the limited space and makes the house look larger than it is.

The hall recurs in a very different guise in **La Saracena**, a villa designed by Luigi Moretti in 1953 in Santa Marinella, Italy. The entrance is wedged between closed masses and an enormous concrete canopy and provides direct access to the hall, which is gradually modulated in height and width. The room eventually looks out over the beach and the Mediterranean. The remarkable elliptical sunken seating area that functions as a dining area reflects the shapes of the exterior in the hall, while at the same time screening a corner with chairs and a hearth from the large continuous space.

English architect Edwin Lutyens was a virtuoso in the use of the passage and the staircase as crucial elements in the spatial design. He designed country houses in a wide variety of historical styles, but behind this stylistic diversity lies a consistent architectural approach in which passages and staircases are the most important elements in terms of both architectural expression and size. The neo-medieval **Drogo Castle** (1910-1930) in Drewsteignton is Lutyens' most impressive country house (and is only a part of the original design, which was on a much grander scale).

In this twentieth-century castle, the staircases and passages occupy considerably more space than the rooms. The plan has two main stairways, the larger of which (the south stairway) encircles a small servants staircase. The route from the main entrance to the dining room on the floor below, and back via the other stairway, is formed by constant changes of direction, affording ever changing views of the interior and exterior, while the ceiling offers a full range of beam constructions, barrel and domed vaulting. As a counterpart to the rambling Drogo Castle, Lutyens' **The Salutation** in Sandwich (1911) achieves the same diversity on a smaller surface area. The hall, staircase and passage to the upper floor of this house in neo-Queen Anne style are constructed from a dozen independently articulated areas on a surface of no more than six by seven metres. The deep incision of the simple rectangular volume on the upper floor to allow light to reach the staircase directly is a brilliant stroke. The hard colours in these areas – black, white, green and blue – reinforce the peculiar character of this spatial implosion.

Lutyens called **Little Thakeham** in Storrington (1902) his favourite design for a country house. In this house, in Arts and Crafts style, the movement has been dramatised by elaborating the complex of stairs in the hall in a capricious classicism,

Vanna Venturi House, Chestnut Hill, Pennsylvania, US

Venturi Scott Brown and Associates

1961

6

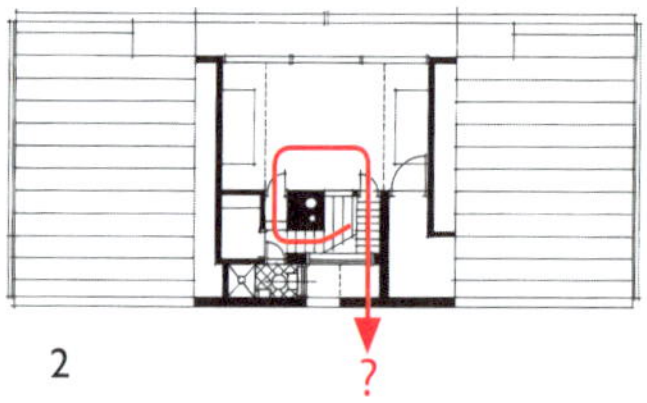

2

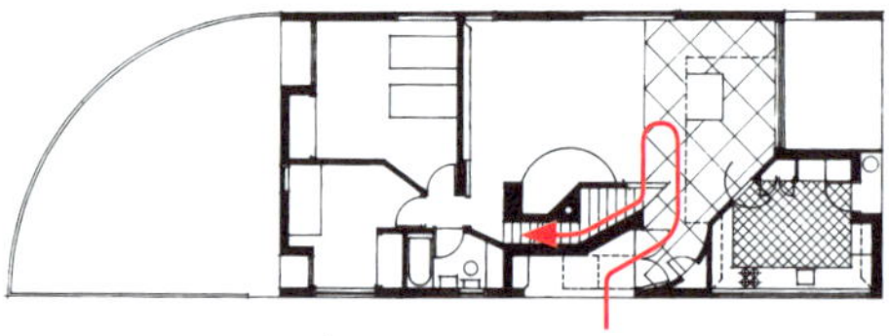

1

5

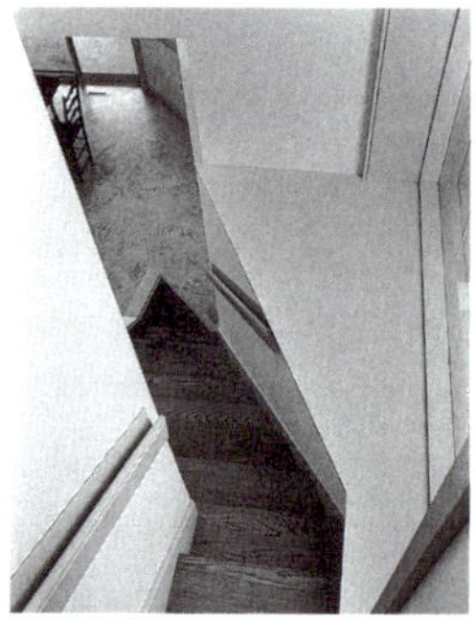

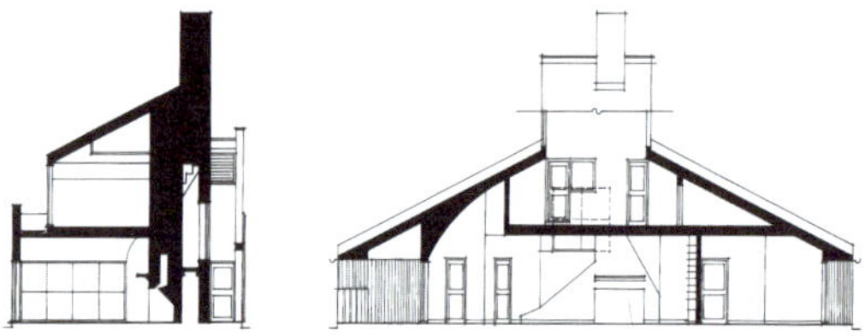

3

1 ground floor
2 top floor
3 cross-sections
4 staircase and hearth
5 staircase from above
6 nowhere stairs in attic

4

Villa La Saracena, Santa Marinella, Rome, Italy
Luigi Moretti
1953–1957

3

4

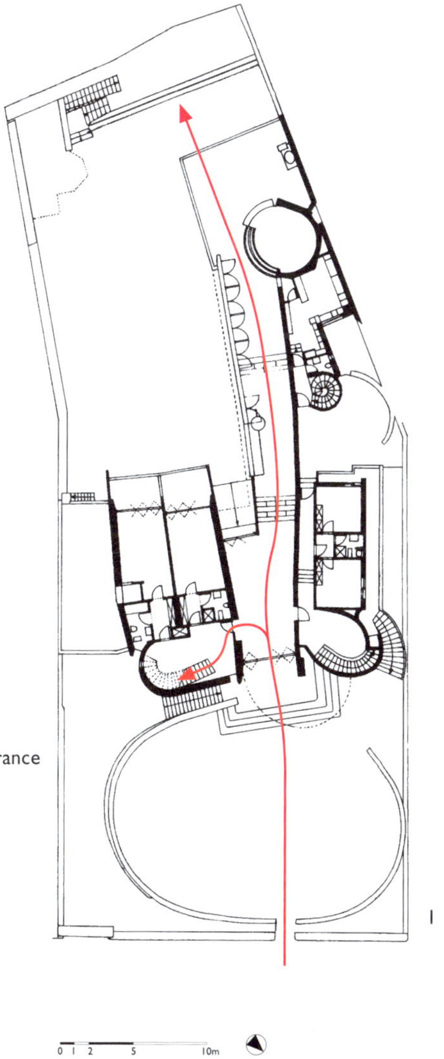

1

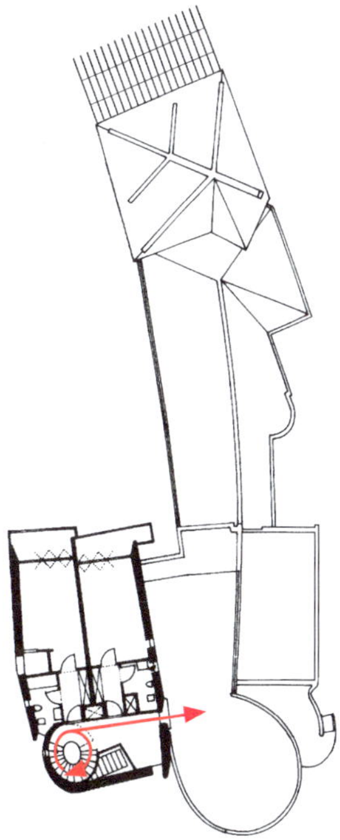

2

1 ground floor
2 first floor
3 house from the street
4 hall looking towards entrance

Drogo Castle, Drewsteignton, Devonshire, UK
Edwin Lutyens
1910–1930

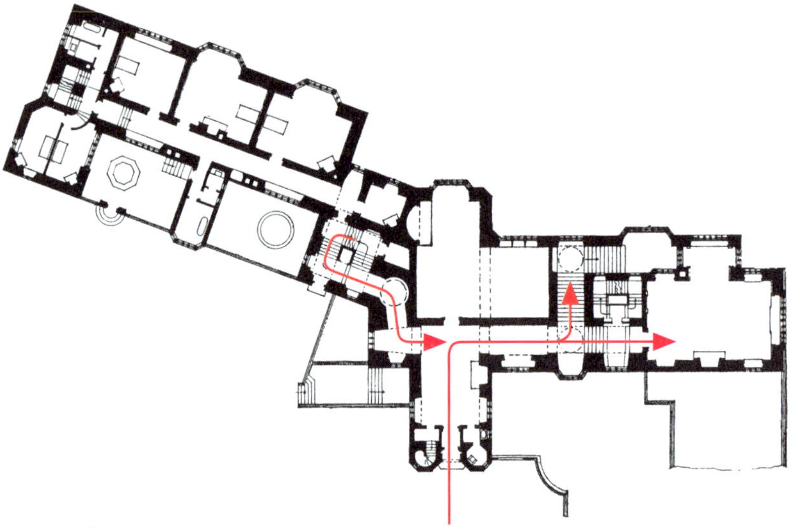

1

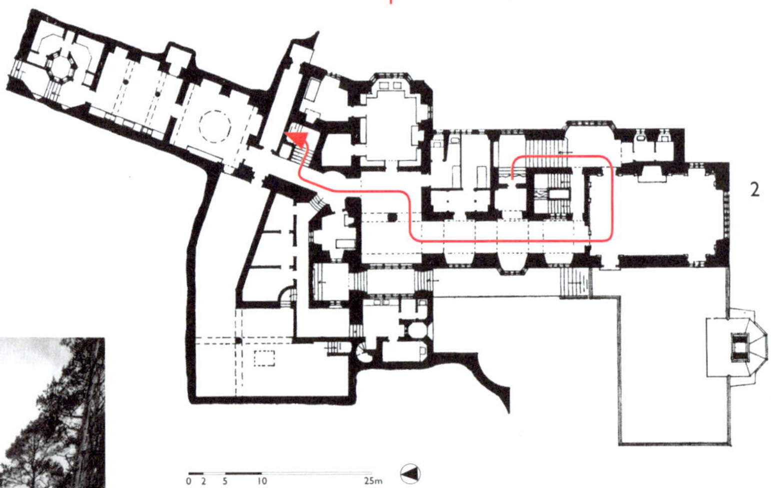

2

3

4

8

10

9

7

5

6

I ground floor
2 lower floor
3 from the south
4 ground floor corridor, northern section
5–6 ground floor corridor, southern section
7 staircase
8–9 stairs to dining room on lower floor
10 lower floor corridor

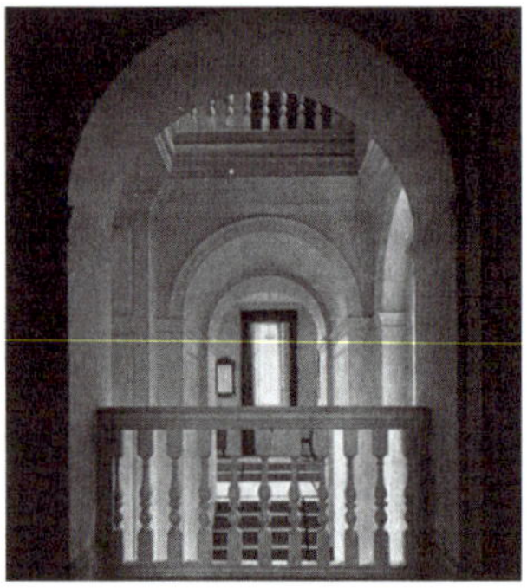

6

The Salutation, Sandwich, Kent, UK

Edwin Lutyens

1911

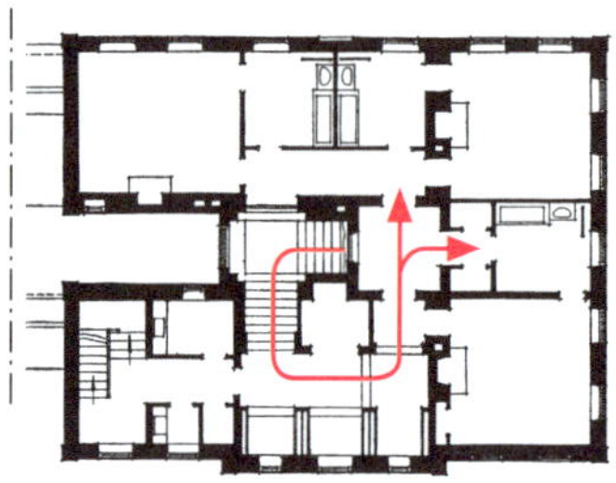

2

4

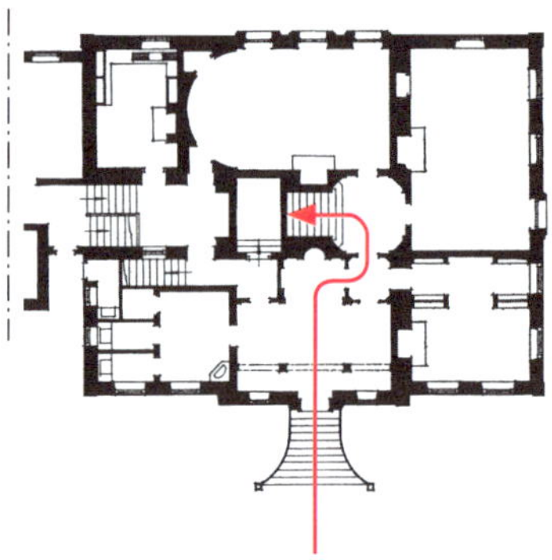

1

5

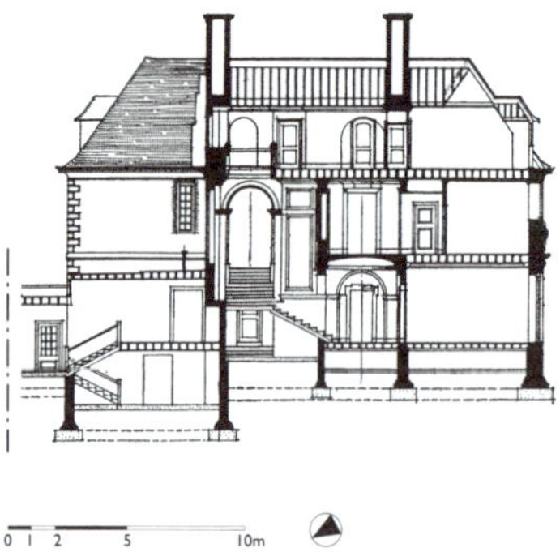

3

1 ground floor
2 first floor
3 cross-section with stairs
4–5 bottom of stairs on ground floor
6 view at first floor level through staircase

Little Thakeham, Storrington, Sussex, UK

Edwin Lutyens

1902

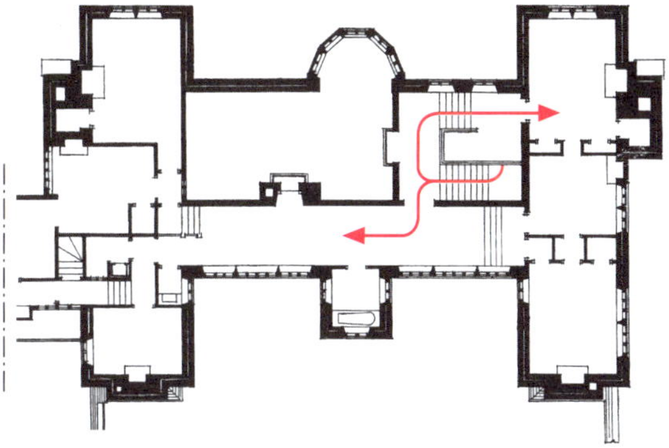

2

3

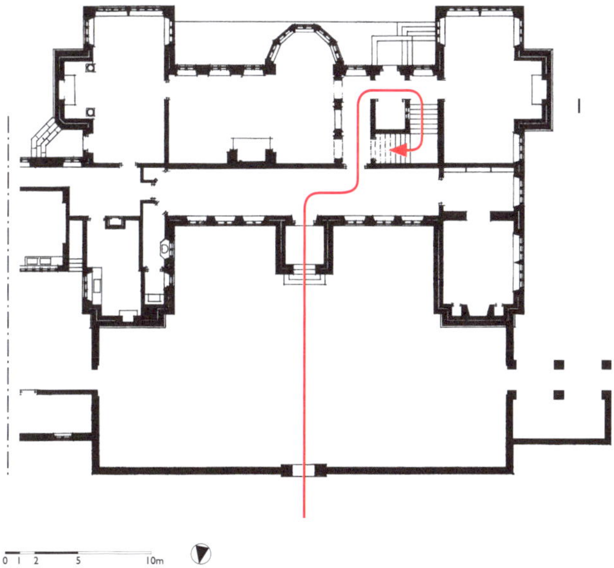

1

1 ground floor
2 first floor
3 hall
4 staircase in living hall

4

while the rest of the interior is highly restrained. As a result, the stairway gives the impression of standing like a piece of décor on an otherwise empty stage.

Like a box at the opera, the corridor on the first floor offers a grandiose view of the hall. This opening has a heavy frame in the same formal idiom as the staircase. The emphatic frame diverts attention from the curious fact that the opening is exactly above the hearth. The chimney has been craftily hidden in the frame.

The sometimes bizarre character of Lutyens' architecture obscures its unique and contemporary spatial design. **Haus Beer** by the Viennese architect Josef Frank, also known as 'the house in the Wenzgasse' (1929–1931), has a spatial design very like that of Lutyens' Little Thakeham. In external appearance, however, Haus Beer is indisputably 'modern', an abstract, plastered box. Like Lutyens' Little Thakeham, the interior presents a theatrical spatiality. In the middle of the house is a hall two floors high that opens directly onto the other rooms. An expressive staircase winds its way upwards in the hall via an open mezzanine with library and music room. The mezzanine, supported by a round column, and the staircase seem to form a piece of décor, though not a Baroque décor, as in Little Thakeham, but modern, or rather, purist, like a fragment of a Corbusian Dom-Ino concrete skeleton in an otherwise traditionally constructed house.

It is particularly this feature which has led many to consider this house as a synthesis of Loos's *Raumplan* (rooms opening directly onto one another at different levels) and Le Corbusier's *plan libre* (open floor surfaces supported by columns that can be divided in a variety of ways).

Frank himself explained the concept of the house in his text *Das Haus als Weg und Platz* [The House as Way and Place], the content of which is clearly summed up in the title. The text describes the spatiality of the English country house, but Frank does not explicitly mention it as a source of inspiration. However, anticipated in this by Le Corbusier, he does refer to the informal spatiality of the artist's studio as such a source. This reference to a bohemian life-style is in line with Frank's opposition to the traditional harmony of space and interior design, and his fondness of freedom and personally determined chaos.

Loos's *Raumplan* concept dissolves the separate circuit, which is absorbed in the rooms. This differs from Lutyens' practice, for the latter turned the circuit into a separate, autonomous element. So the English country house seems to have inspired two mutually conflicting spatial organisations: a model in which the circuit forms an autonomous and dominant part; and a model in which the circuit is entirely absorbed by the rooms.

The absorption of the circuit by the rooms had already been introduced in the United States before the development of the *Raumplan*. The concept of the home as a continuous space gained ground faster there because architects in the US were less bothered by the historical ballast of the European design tradition. Frank Lloyd Wright's early villas already display a strong fixation on movement through the house, which is accompanied in his work by a minimising of the distinction between rooms and circuit.

In his early homes, Wright developed a number of fixed patterns that recur in all the later work, irrespective of programme and dimension: the main rooms are fused together, and only the rooms that cannot be open are placed in the space as rudimentary masses. The circuit seems to have disappeared in these designs, but the movement through the space is nevertheless determined by the position of the closed masses.

The large number of homes that Wright produced follow this design almost without exception. The Usonian homes of the 1930s, which Wright regarded as prototypes for the ideal suburban home, are exemplary. **The Stanley Rosenbaum House** in Florence, Alabama, is a typical Usonian design: an open ground plan on one floor, divided into a living room, dining room, study and three bedrooms by cupboards, a hearth, and a closed volume containing the kitchen, toilet and a second fireplace.

The idea of an open ground plan but one that is highly structured in functional terms was particularly investigated by many architects in the 1940s and 1950s. There is an unusual example in the work of Hugo Häring. In the ground plan of a **single-storey house** (1946) that was never built, the spatial articulation is entirely determined by an optimisation of the routes between the different components of the programme. Häring used the word *Leistungsform* [purposive form] in this connection.

The consequences of a ground plan in which the rooms and circuit coincide were also explored in a number of conceptual designs by Alison and Peter Smithson: **The Appliance House**. These plans aimed at a home as a single space incorporating separate units for the genuinely privacy-sensitive rooms and to accommodate the domestic appliances whose numbers were increasing significantly at the time. The Retirement House, designed for The Homestead in Hawkhurst (1959), displays an affinity with Wright's Usonian homes; sketch plans like the Snowball House and the Cubicle House extrude the utilities units, thereby creating a kind of wall around an open central space. In this respect the sketch for the Cubicle House shows a striking resemblance to the ground plan of Dover Castle from eight centuries earlier.

The return to this model is connected with the changed programme of the home. The separation between public and private rooms had already lost much of its relevance after the First World War, and the wave of democratisation that followed in the aftermath of the Second World War even called the passage into

Haus Beer, Vienna, Austria
Josef Frank
1929–1931

5

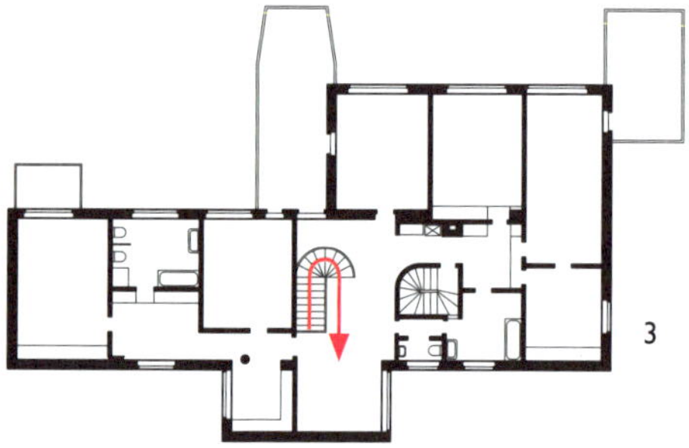

3

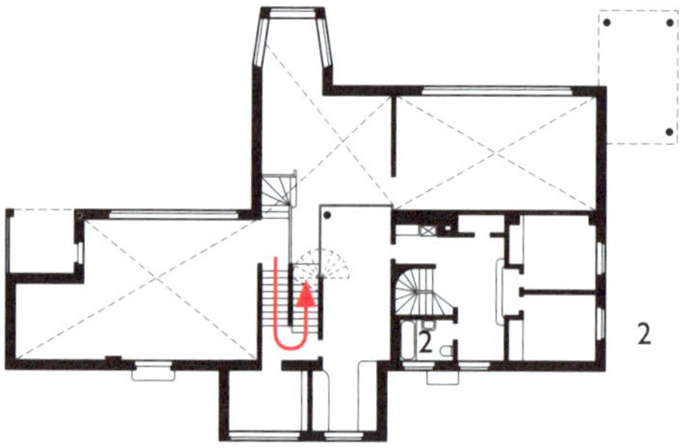

2

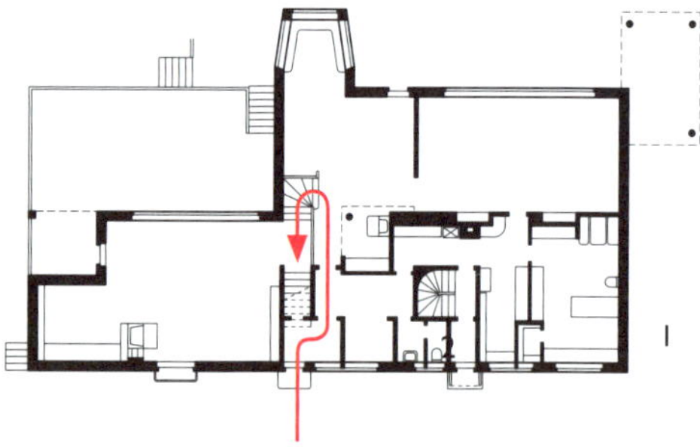

I

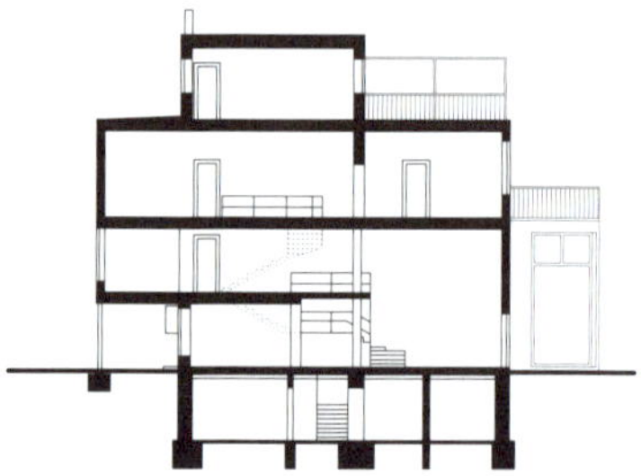

4

I ground floor
2 mezzanine
3 first floor
4 cross-section with hall
5 façade, street side
6–9 hall with mezzanine

6

7

8

9

Stanley Rosenbaum House, Florence, Alabama, US

Frank Lloyd Wright

1939–1940

4

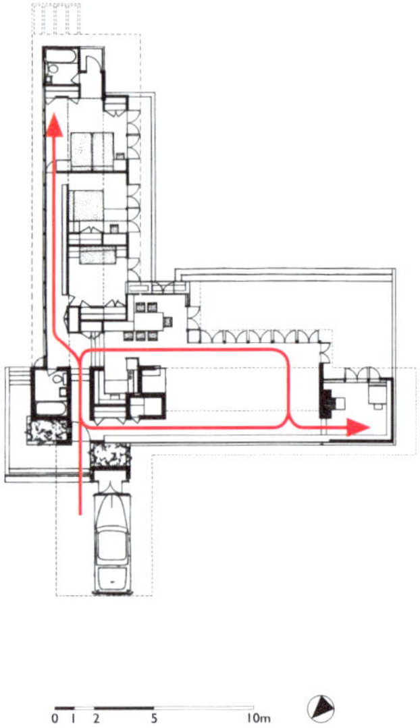

1

2

3

1 ground floor
2 street side
3 garden side
4 sitting room

Design for a house, project
Hugo Häring
1946

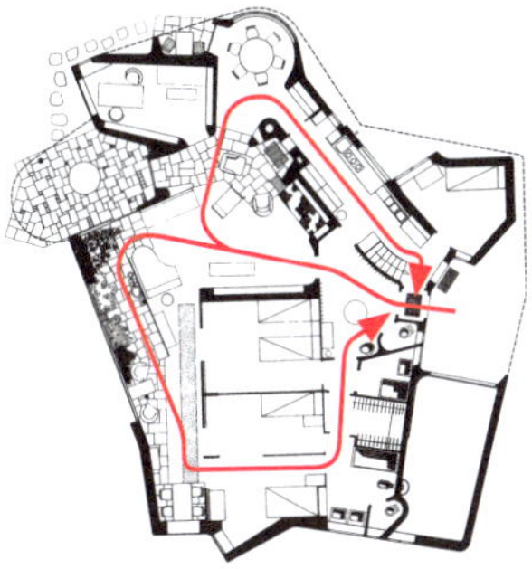
1

I ground floor
2 east façade

2
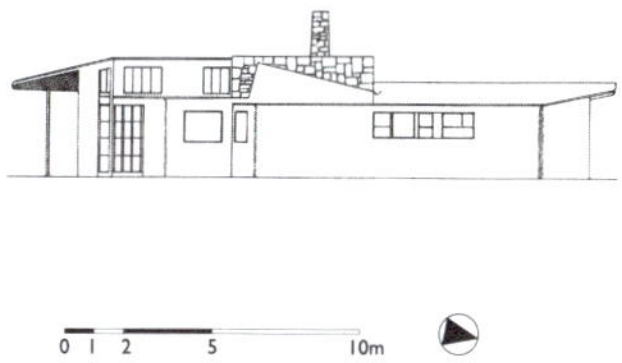

The Appliance House
Alison and PeterSmithson
1956–1959

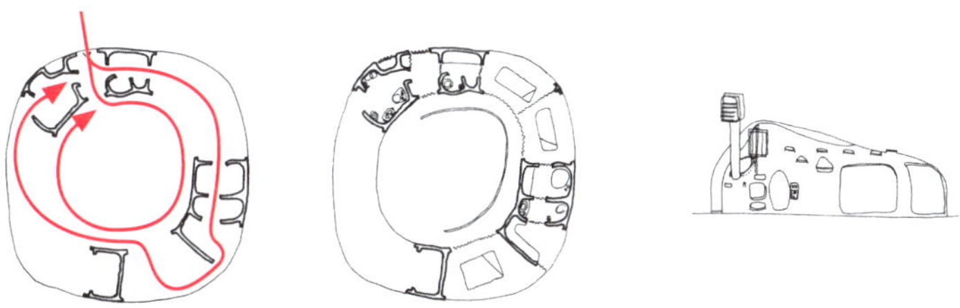
1

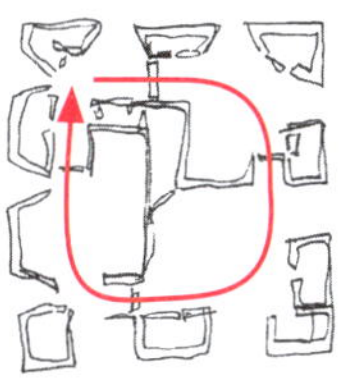
2

3
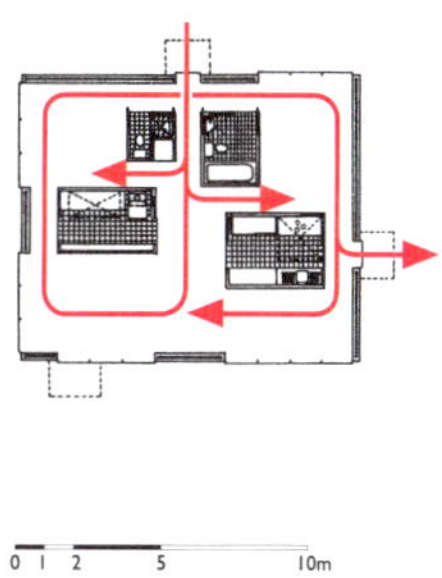

I sketches of Snowball House
2 sketch of Cubicle House
3 the Retirement House (the Homestead, Hawkhurst, Kent, UK)

question, especially in public and industrial buildings. Whereas the passage had functioned for centuries as the intermediary between private and public, from the 1970s on the corridor was increasingly seen as an obstacle to social contact. The English historian of architecture Robin Evans, for instance, published an article in *Architectural Design* in 1978 that can be read as an anti-corridor manifesto. He described the development of the 'corridor plan' as 'a general lobotomy performed on society at large, obliterating vast areas of social experience'. The article is a plea for social interaction by connecting rooms with one another. The article is not an isolated phenomenon; it is part of the revival of the open ground plan in all kinds of buildings, but especially in offices, where the office garden and the *Bürolandschaft* became the rage.

In 1971 Norman Foster designed the **Willis, Faber & Dumas** office building in Ipswich. It has a fully open structure in which elevators link the levels without walls. The elevators do bring out the movement through the building, but there is no further spatial differentiation. It is thus a reflection of ideas like those advocated by Evans: architecture in an open, democratic society should not be hierarchical. It is characteristic that the directors' rooms do not occupy a prominent place and that the elevators lead to the canteen on the top floor. The canteen and the swimming pool on the ground floor constitute the main social space of the office building.

Almost every exponent of this ideal, from De Meerpaal in Dronten by Frank van Klingeren, and Herman Hertzberger's office for Centraal Beheer in Apeldoorn from the late 1960s, to MVRDV's Villa VPRO in Hilversum from the 1990s, has proved to be controversial. Time after time, it turned out to be difficult to accommodate pluriform programmes in a large, undivided space, which underlines the relevance of the corridor all the more.

Because most of today's homes are a good deal less complicated than the country houses that were built at the beginning of the twentieth century, the spatial and functional significance of the corridor in the home has usually been limited.

For buildings with complex programmes, however, the corridor still has a great importance in all its forms and properties. Models that are used in homes are often also applicable to other types of buildings. That this does not have to lead to a literal adaptation can be seen from Denys Lasdun's **Royal College of Physicians** overlooking Regent's Park (1959). Like Hardwick Hall, it is based on a continuous route connecting rooms that are to a greater or lesser extent open to the public. The central hall is like a heart whose blood circulates through the arteries of the corridors. Lasdun deliberately chose this metaphor because it was a famous seventeenth-century member of the College of Physicians, William Harvey, who discovered the circulation of the blood.

Four hundred years after Hardwick, a similar route can be found in the design for the **Dutch Embassy** in Berlin by OMA/Rem Koolhaas. Far more than in Hardwick Hall, the route – a *trajectory* in the terminology of OMA, and presented in that form as a new invention – leaves its mark on the entire building as its cuts its way through nine floors. This route also establishes a strong link between the building and its surroundings by offering new views at each turn. The continuous route linking all the rooms and the large degree of transparency, however, are at odds with the security of embassies today.

Another example of a (semi-)public building in which the movement has a structuring effect is the **Edifício da Reitoria** of the University of Brasiliá, designed in 1972 by Paolo Zimbres. Despite its appearance as an amorphous mass, spatial clarity is introduced to the building by linking the circuit with the rooms. In the heart of the building staircases and ramps connect large patios with a number of more or less public rooms, such as lecture halls. Because the staircases and ramps directly overlook the patios, they form a link between indoor and outdoor space. As a result, movement through the space inside the building passes seamlessly into movement through the space outside the building. This blurs the distinction between inside and outside, thereby causing the building to recede into the background, an effect that is reinforced by the luxuriant vegetation in the patios, which are inhabited by birds and monkeys. Mass and space have both been forced to assume a secondary role; the leading role is for the movement through the space and for the transition from indoors to outdoors through the mass of the architecture.

Willis Faber & Dumas Building, Ipswich, UK

Norman Foster

1971–1975

5

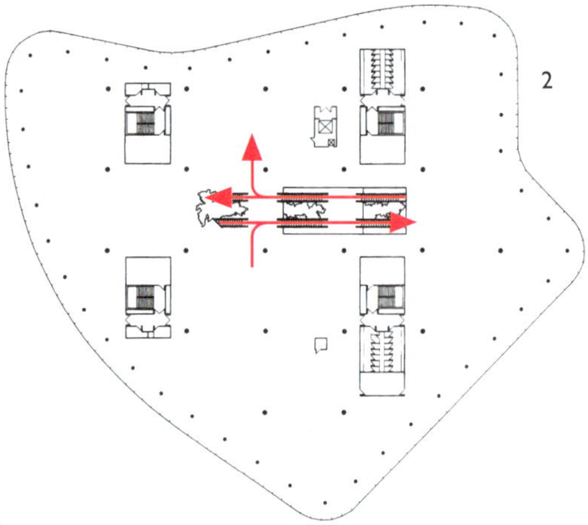

2

I ground floor
2 second floor
3 cross-section with escalators
4 central open space with escalators
5 top floor with restaurant and lawn

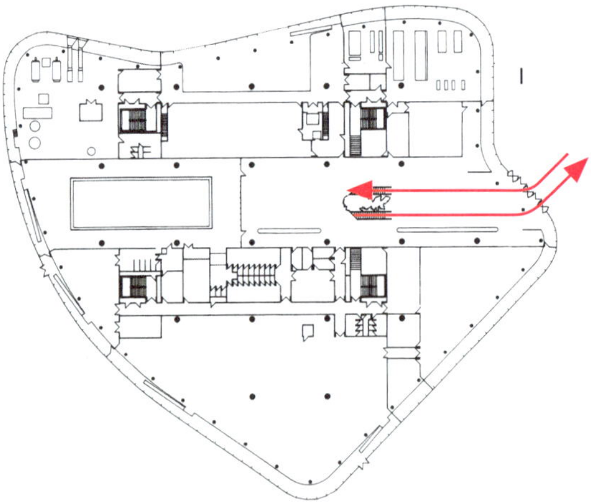

I

4

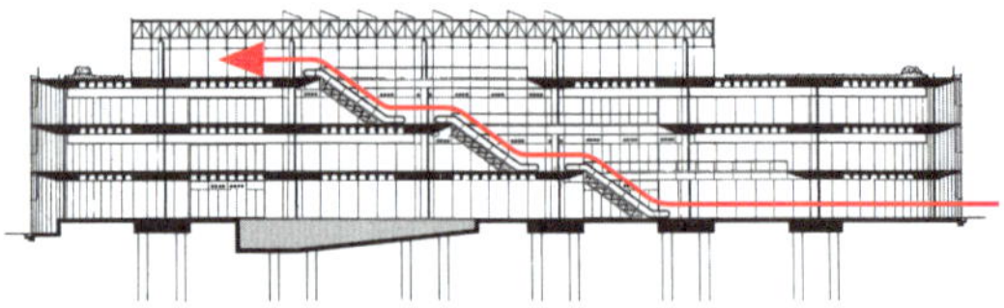

3

6

Royal College of Physicians, Regents Park, London, UK
Denys Lasdun
1959

1
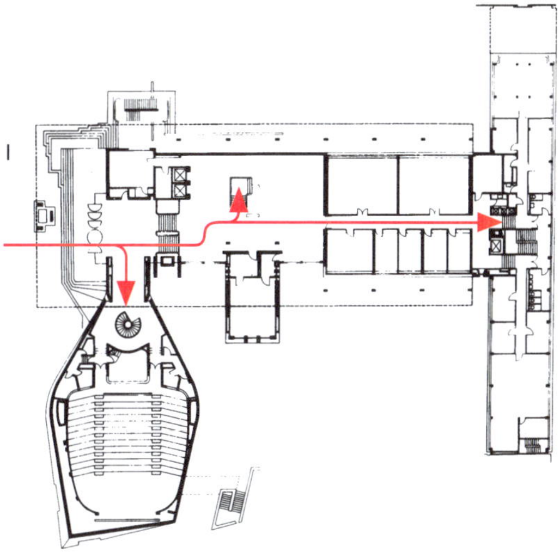

2
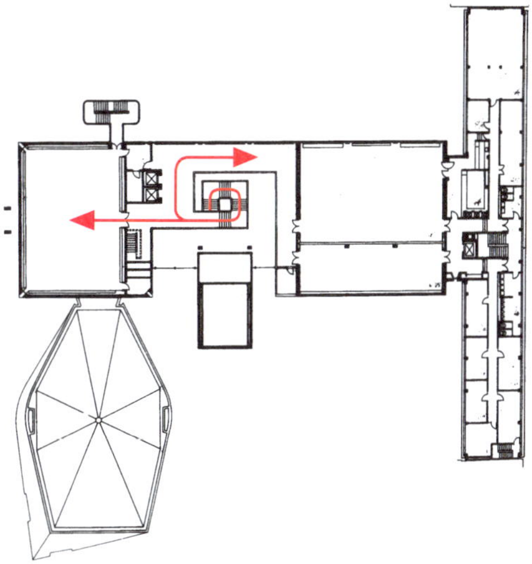

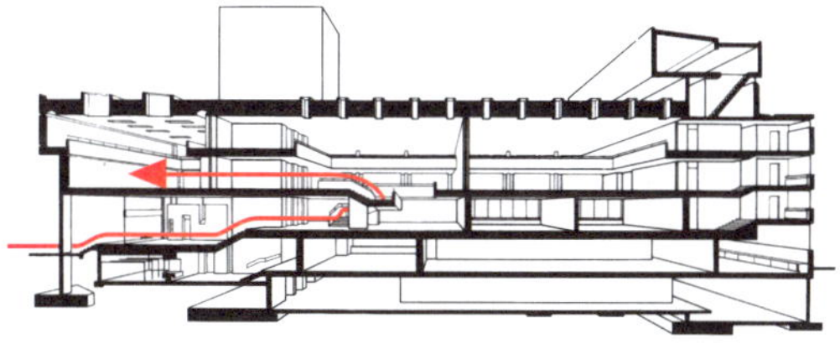

3

5

1 ground floor
2 first floor
3 cross-section of central hall
4 staircase seen from ground floor
5 staircase seen from second floor
6 first floor corridor

4

Dutch Embassy, Berlin, Germany
OMA/Rem Koolhaas
1997–2003

7

6

1 level 1, +3.70 metres
2 level 3, +8.65 metres
3 level 6, +14.25 metres
4 level 9, +20.50 meters
5 façade, street side
6–7 trajectory

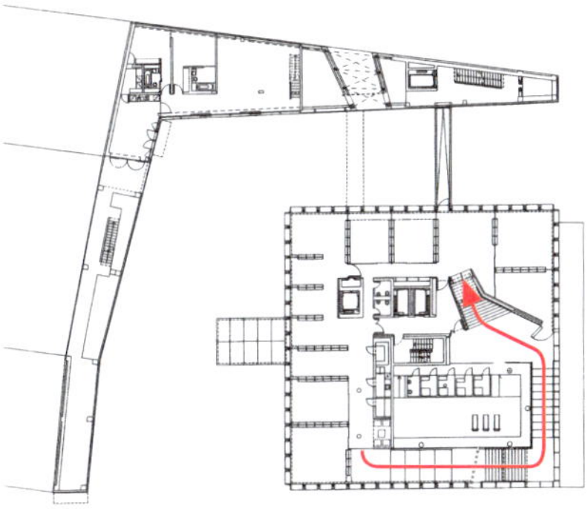

4

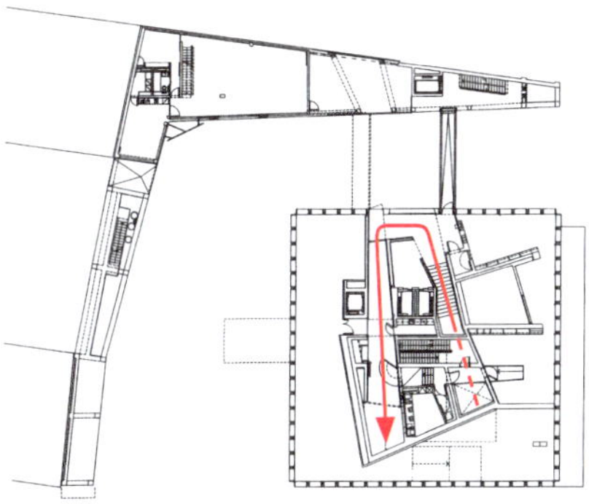

3

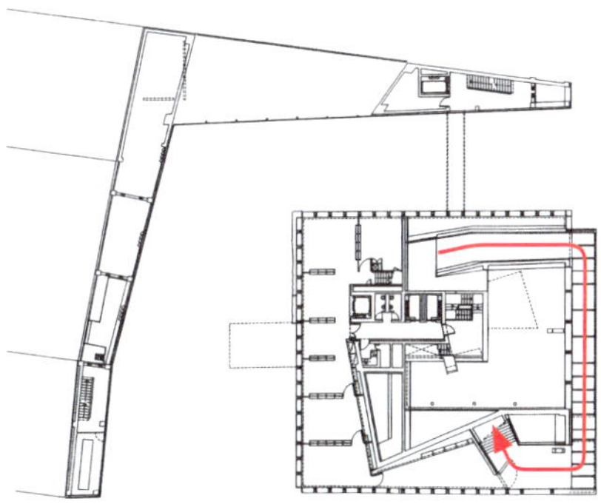

2

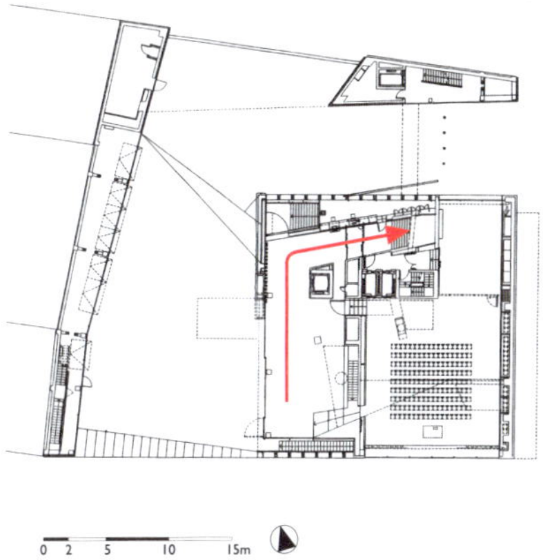

1

5

Edifício da Reitoria, Brasiliá, Brazil
Paolo Zimbres
1972–1975

6

7

8

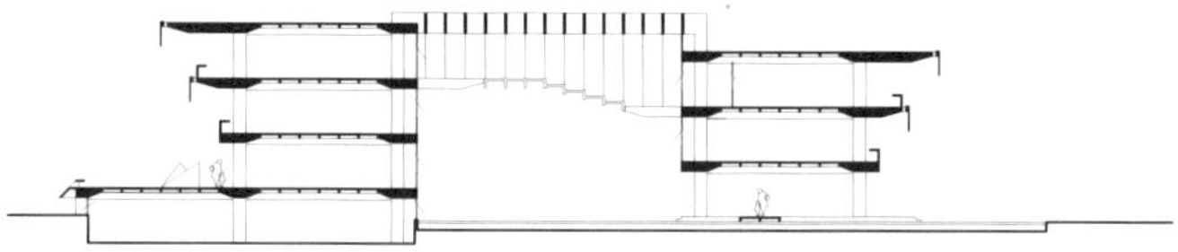
4

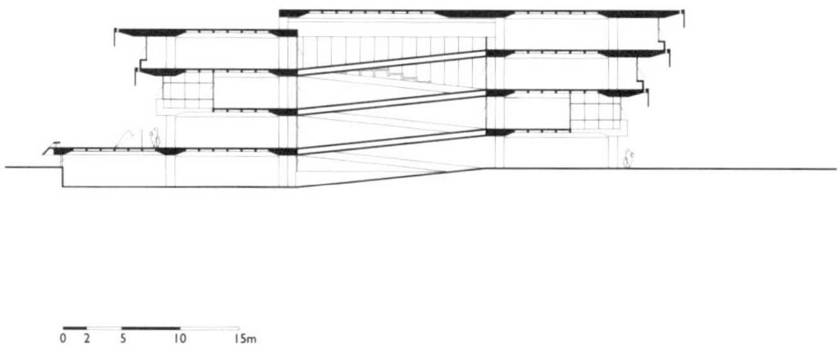
5

9

1 ground floor
2 third floor
3 fifth floor
4 cross-section over patio
5 cross-section over ramp
6 outside
7 central zone building with patios
8–10 patios with stairs and ramps

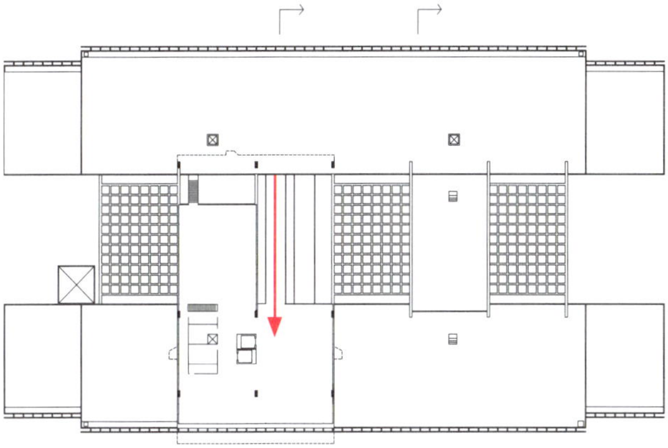

3

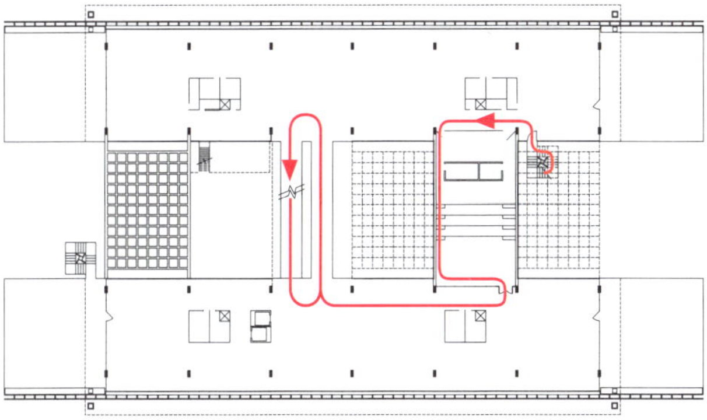

2

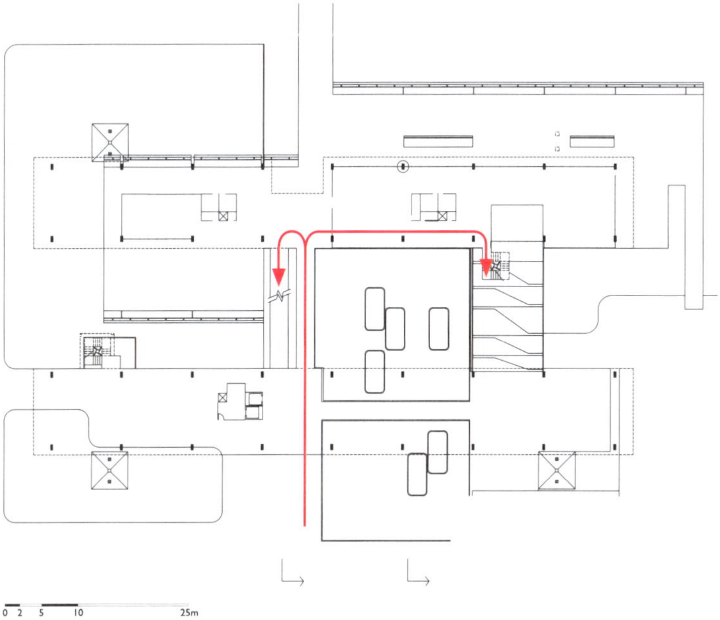

1

10

The corridor enables spaces that are occupied and used in very different ways to coexist. This makes it an important spatial instrument to reconcile privacy, diversity and density within one and the same building. Thanks to its functional neutrality, the passage can also confer a permanent programmatic flexibility on a building.

A far-reaching intertwining of circuit and utilitarian space can greatly enhance the spatial quality and complexity of the design, but can also endanger its functional quality. The exact position of the corridor and the balance between connection and separation are crucial.

A number of principles of corridor design have been tried out in six housing projects. These are homes in which the movement unambiguously defines the spatial characteristic of the home, vertically or horizontally. In four of the designs for utilitarian programmes, the confrontation of several user functions and patterns of movement lead to spatial structures of greater complexity. By developing and articulating each pattern separately, these designs retain a functional clarity.

R R R

R R R

R R R

1 Canalside house, Java Island, Amsterdam

This house is one of a series built along the canals of the Java Island in Amsterdam. Within the prescribed structure of tunnels of reinforced concrete, an attempt has been made to create a maximum of spatial freedom in order to escape the rigidity of this building system. This has resulted in a house in which all the rooms of varying height interlock. The rooms are connected by a continuous staircase whose position changes per level. There is a six-metre-high living room on the first floor, while the top floor contains a high studio that also receives light through the roof via a patio.

9

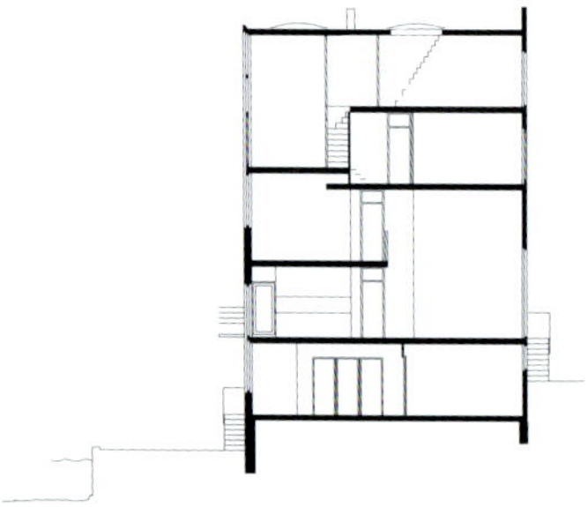

7

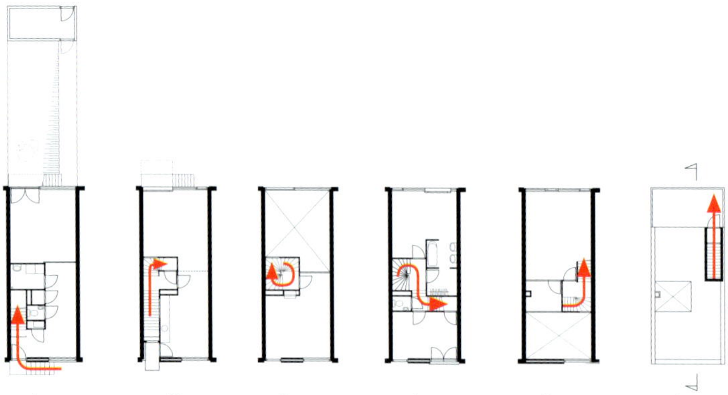

1 2 3 4 5 6

8

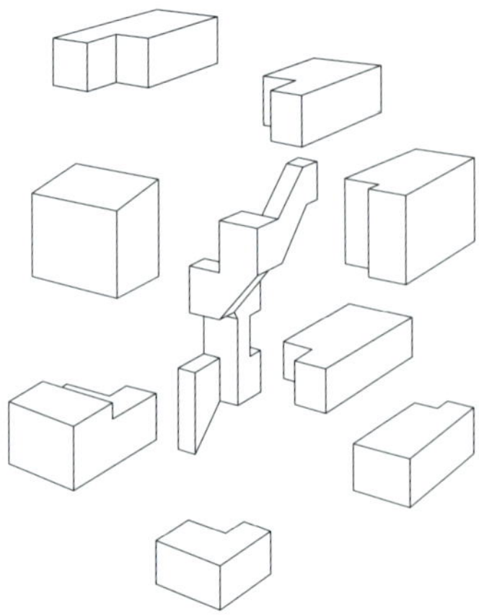

10

11

1 entrance level
2 living room level
3 mezzanine
4 bedroom level and studio
5 attic level
6 roof with terrace
7 section
8 spaces around staircase
9 façade on canal side
10 studio
11 façade on the rear side
12 mezzanine

12

11 Private house, Valeriusstraat, Amsterdam

In a typical Amsterdam house, built around 1900, the interior of the lower half of the building, which extends over three floors, has been renovated. The characteristic narrow, deep structure of the house, consisting of two elongated rectangles separated by a supporting wall on each floor, has been maintained: a wider one for the rooms, and a narrower one for the corridor. By making openings in the floors of the corridors, a nine-metre-high vertical hall connecting all the rooms in the house has been created in the narrower rectangle. Where the floor has been cut away, the former door openings function as windows onto the hall. The wider rectangle has been left as open as possible. The bathroom on the first floor has been designed as a piece of furniture that separates the two bedrooms without marring the continuous space. All of the lateral walls in the house have been removed, and some of them have been replaced by glass partitions, so that the light can penetrate everywhere into the heart of the house.

8

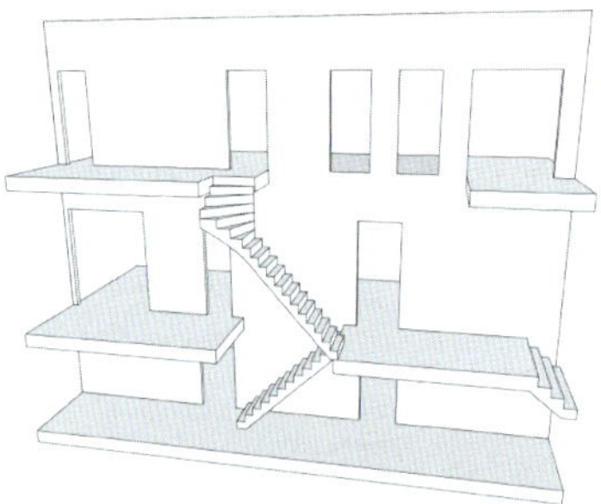

5

9

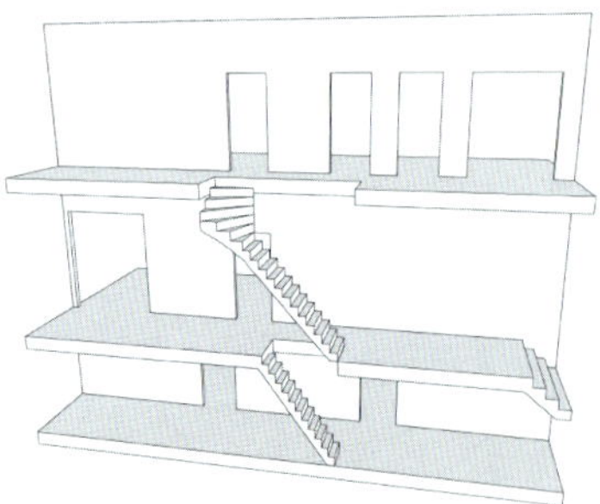

10

6

7

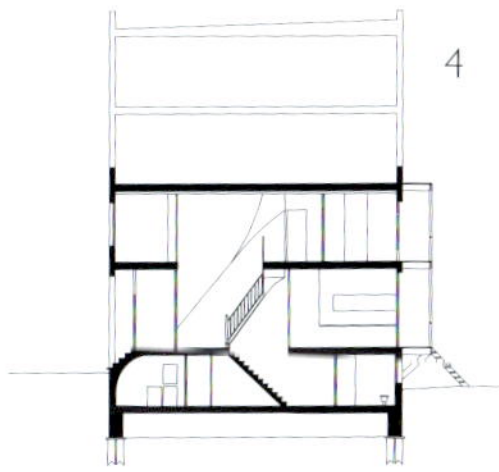

4

1 basement
2 ground floor
3 first floor
4 cross-section
5 narrow section before and after renovation
6 hall seen from vestibule
7 hall seen from first floor
8 living room
9 bedroom on garden side with wardrobe
10 bathroom

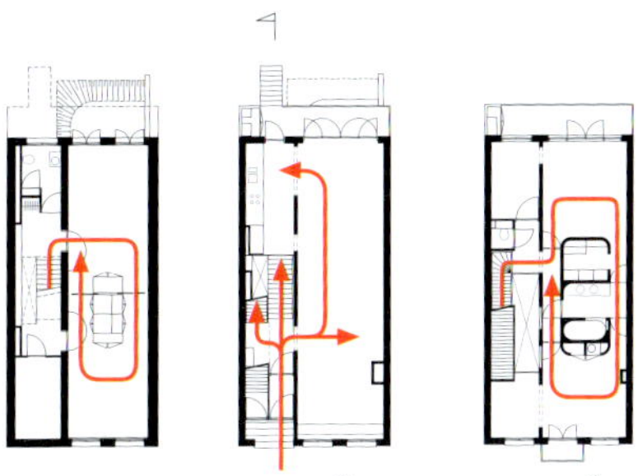

1 2 3

III House, Borneo Island, Amsterdam

The house-cum-studio in the Scheepstimmermanstraat is one of a series of sixty individually developed housing units on the Borneo Island in Amsterdam. It is on a small plot, wedged between two neighbours, with the street at the front and a former mooring dock at the rear. Within a width of a mere 3.80 metres, a large programme has been achieved for a low budget: a one-family home, a studio, and a parking space that had to be incorporated on the site. The maximum permitted volume was required to create enough square metres for all the functions. The only empty space in the volume consists of two shafts to allow light to enter, one with a ground surface area of 1 by 1 metres, the other with a ground surface area of 2 by 2 metres, which allow daylight to enter the 16-metre deep interior. Two independent circulation systems have been created in the limited volume. A series of continuous flights of stairs leads from the street to the studio on the top floor. The second route is a combination of a ramp, a spiral staircase and a straight staircase that connect the private rooms distributed over the three floors.

7

10

11

8

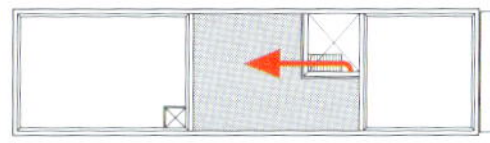

5

4

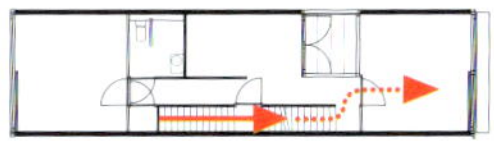

3

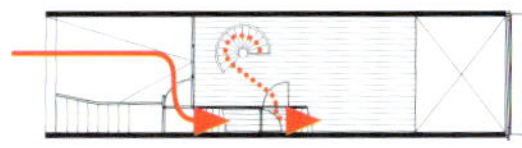

2

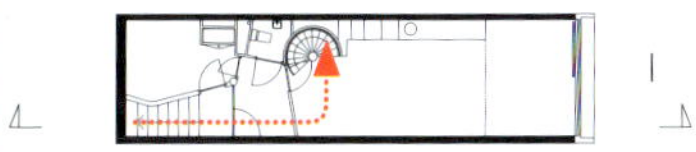

1

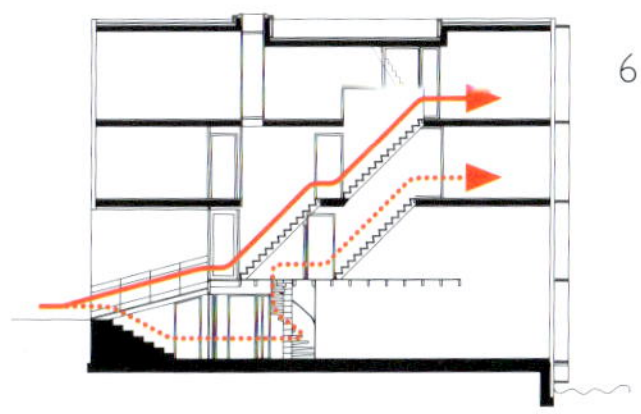

6

9

1 basement

2 intermediate level

3 bedroom level

4 studio

5 rooftop level

6 cross-section

7 street side

8 rear overlooking water

9 intermediate level

10–11 studio

IV Apartment, end of Borneo Island, Amsterdam

The apartment is on the top floor at the end of a block with 57 housing units on the Borneo Island in Amsterdam. In accordance with the stipulations of West 8 in the urban design for this area, the block consists of ground-level homes. Only the end of the block, facing the open water, did not have to abide by these regulations. Here the pattern of ground-level units has been abandoned, and three different apartments have been created within the structure of concrete tunnels. After the dimensions of the tunnels had been fixed, a half-tunnel was left over at the end of the block. This has been made as a half tunnel of exposed concrete, which functions as a terrace, so that the building structure that is covered with bricks elsewhere is exposed here. The terraces accommodate a number of glass rooms in delicate balance, as a rudiment of what might otherwise have been the interior of a complete tunnel. The interior design for the topmost apartment changed the original design of four separate rooms and a corridor proposed by the project developer into an open space lit from all four sides. A central core area contains all the sanitary facilities and the kitchen. The core is positioned to create a sequence of alternating extroverted and introverted areas. In spite of the open character of the façades, the apartment as a whole has a closed character. The overhanging terrace hides life in the apartment from the view of the street; at the same time, the largely transparent outer walls afford an unobstructed panoramic view of the water.

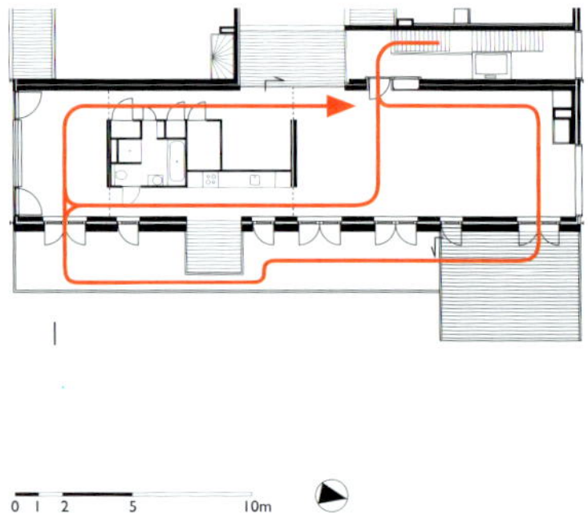

4

5

3

1 plan of end apartment, second floor
2 end of block
3 terrace with glass rooms
4 core with kitchen
5 living space

2

V Apartment beside the Singel, Amsterdam

The apartment is situated in a seventeenth-century warehouse. Almost all of the partition walls have been removed. A volume containing the bathroom, kitchen, dining table and cupboards has been placed in the centre of the empty space. Since this volume touches neither walls nor ceiling, daylight can reach far into the apartment. Part of one side of the bathroom, which is in the middle of the volume, is made of sanded glass to admit daylight as well. The outer wall of the volume consists mainly of storage space, with the kitchen facing the side wall. Sliding doors separate the bedroom from the rest of the apartment. These doors, as well as the dining table, are concealed in the walls of the volume.

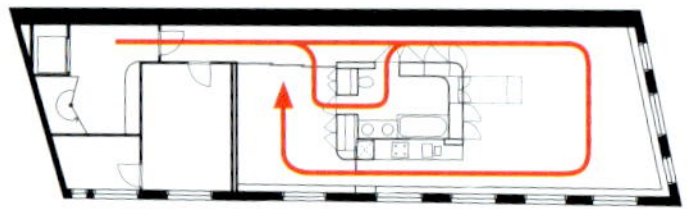

1

5

2

3

4

1 ground plan
2 central volume with unfolded table
3 bathroom
4 kitchen
5 corridor zone

VI Apartment in former sewage treatment plant, Amsterdam

This apartment is part of a project in the Oostoever district, which has sprung up on the site of a former sewage treatment plant in West Amsterdam. The apartment extends over the top floor of a block of seven housing units in a pierced concrete drum that was formerly used as a sediment reservoir. The topmost apartment peeps above the edge of the cylinder, and enjoys a panoramic view thanks to the completely glass façades. To protect the residents of the apartment from the gaze of the neighbours in the adjoining apartment buildings, a very introverted hall has been created in the middle of the apartment. All the other rooms are accessed from this hall, which receives daylight through the roof. The doors immediately next to the outer walls provide a second circuit through the apartment, independently of the hall.

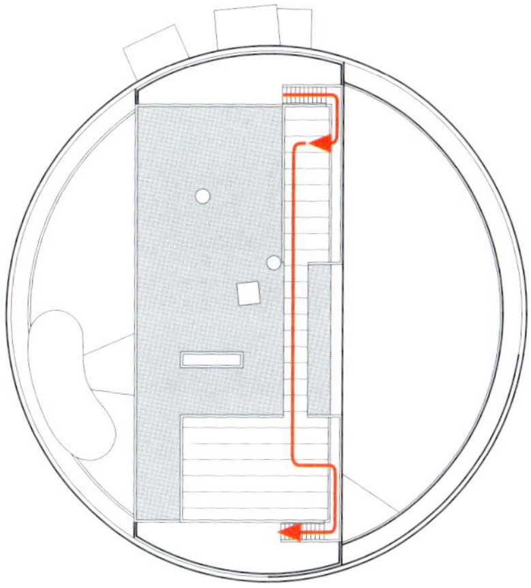

2

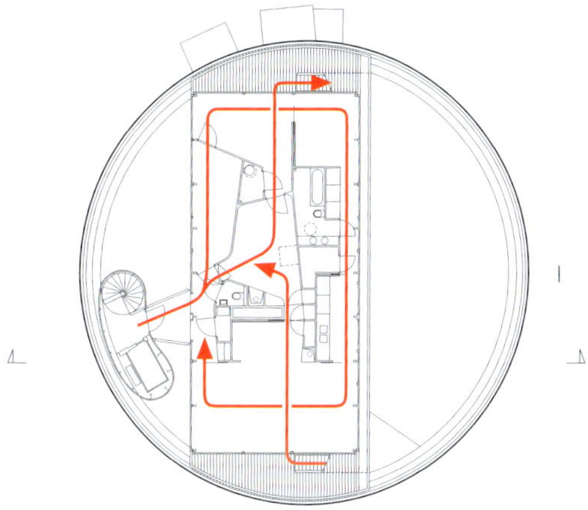

1

4

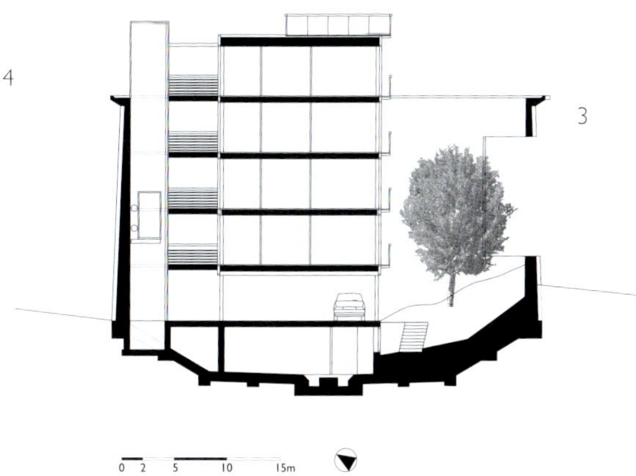

3

5

1 ground plan
2 roof terrace
3 cross-section
4 interior hall
5 exterior

VII Office building, Steenwijk

The office, designed for a housing association and after completion taken over by a firm of engineers, is situated at the tip of one of the green canals around the centre of Steenwijk. The construction consists of a house of cards of concrete wedges; the walls change direction on each floor. As a result, the central hall for employees on the first floor is rotated in relation to the hall for the public on the ground floor. Four shafts in the middle of the building link all of the levels with one another. A stairway winds through the largest of these shafts from the areas for the public on the ground floor to the restaurant and conference room on the second floor, overlooking the centre of Steenwijk. The offices of the employees are located on the first floor, beside corridors that encircle the two central shafts. Between these two shafts is a hall that provides a shortcut between these circuits and is also connected, by means of a second staircase, with the reception areas for clients on the ground floor.

5

6

1 ground floor
2 first floor
3 second floor
4 cross-section
5 entrance side
6 working space on the ground floor
7 corridor, first floor
8 staircase connecting the public areas

7

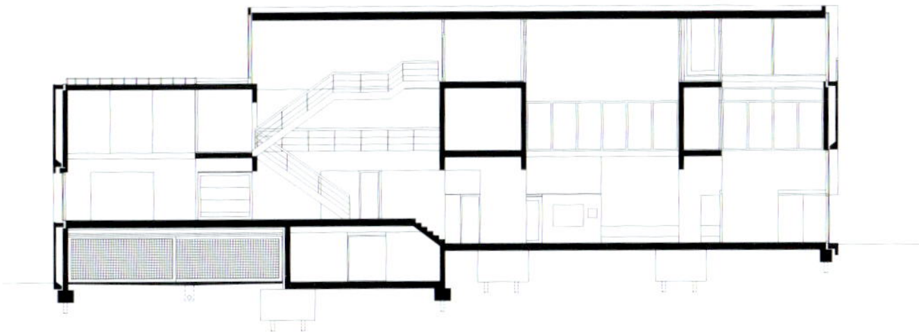

4

8

1

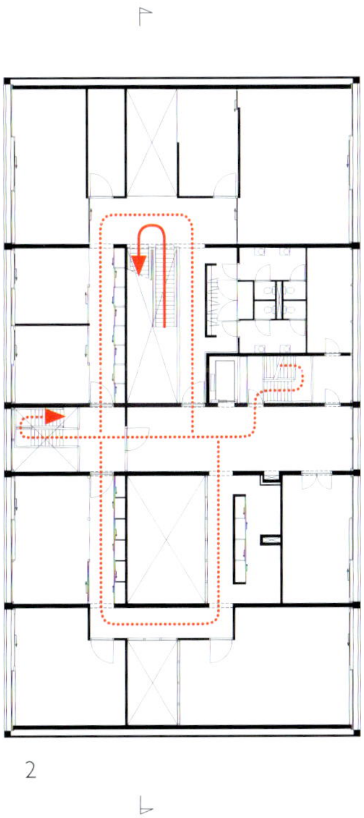

2

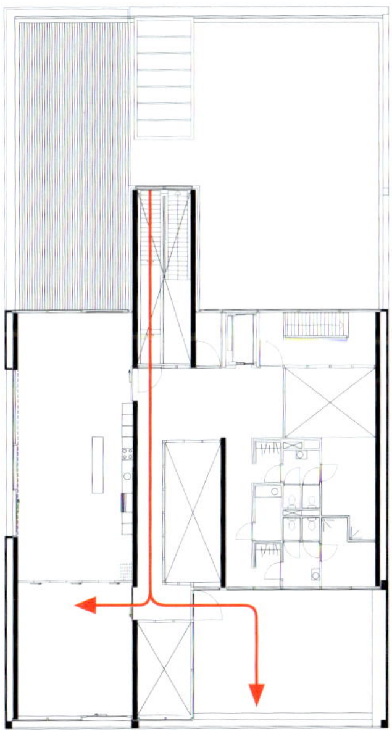

3

2

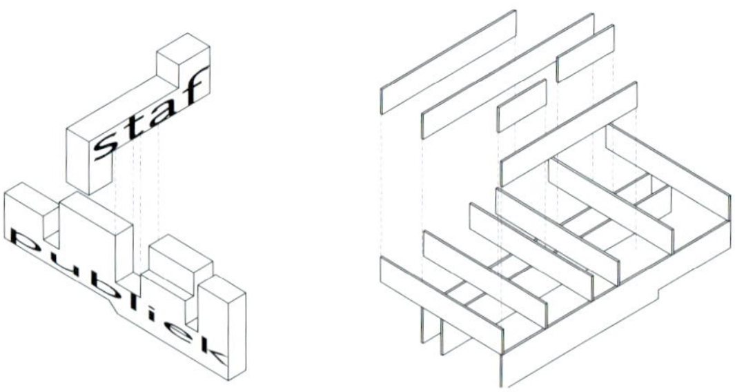

1

3

1 spatial and structural diagram
2 west façade beside water
3 rear hall
4 entrance hall

4

VIII Dutch Embassy, Adis Abeba, Ethiopia

The site of the Dutch embassy on the outskirts of Adis Abeba consists of five hectares of eucalyptus woods, dropping steeply into a valley. The historic villa on the edge of the site has been expanded, while the embassy and residence of the ambassador, three homes for members of staff and the entrance are new. The new buildings blend with the landscape, with a winding road as the connecting element. The gatehouse, camouflaged in the colours of the Dutch flag, peers over the wall on the street side. The extension of the villa, which is occupied by the Vice Ambassador, has been placed beneath the existing house, which now seems to float above the garden. The three homes for staff are situated behind a wall, next to the wall that surrounds the site. The difference in gradient means that they are placed one behind the other like terraces, and that all residents enjoy an unobstructed view. The embassy with ambassador's residence is situated in the centre of the terrain in a long, horizontal volume that seems to have been carved out of the landscape, like a traditional Ethiopian church carved out of the rock. The outside walls are of rough concrete in the same red colour as the ground. The landscape intersects the volume on the borderline of the two functions. At this point the road embedded in the landscape passes over the building, before dropping to the covered visitors entrance of the residence. The roof, that comes into sight at the moment that the road intersects the building, has been implemented as a shallow pond, a reference to the Netherlands in the uneven Ethiopian landscape. The embassy is simple in structure, with offices on either side of a central corridor. This corridor rises with the gradient of the site. The entrance is situated at the lowest point of the corridor, at the end. There is enough space here for an intermediate level, where the ambassador's office is situated. It is connected via a stairway to the rooftop path leading to the residence.

6

7

1 lower level of chancellery and residence
2 upper level of chancellery and residence
3 roof
4 cross-section
5 cross-section of middle zone with corridor and patio
6 roof landscape
7 entrance to the residence
8 chancellery in progress

The residence has two storeys. The upper floor contains the formal reception rooms, while the lower one contains the private rooms. Light shafts and patios link the areas inside and outside the building. As a result of the difference in gradient of the site, both floors are at ground level, so that they can be used entirely independently of one another. Three concealed stairways – one for the ambassador, one for his family, and one for staff – form the internal routes between the floors.

8

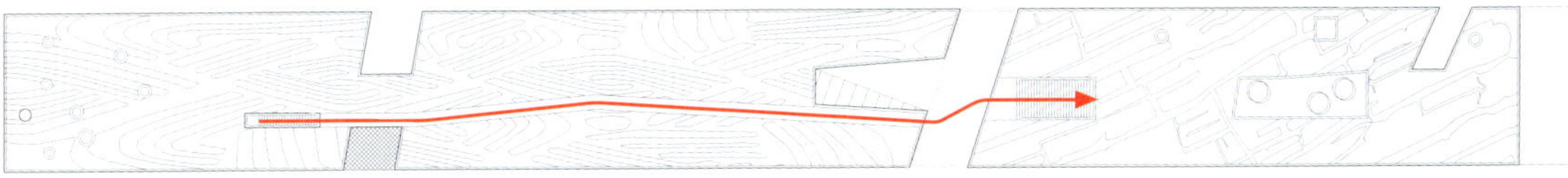

3

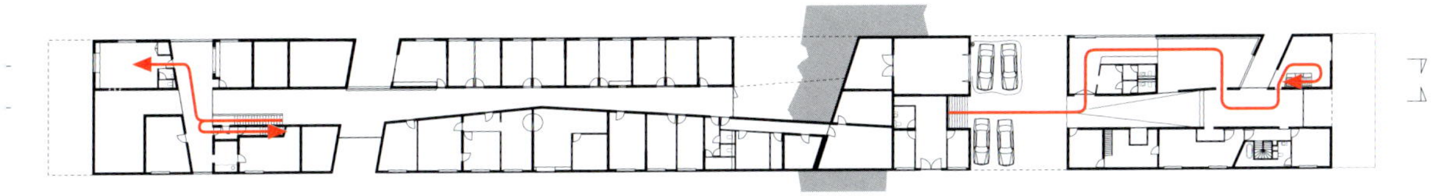

2

1

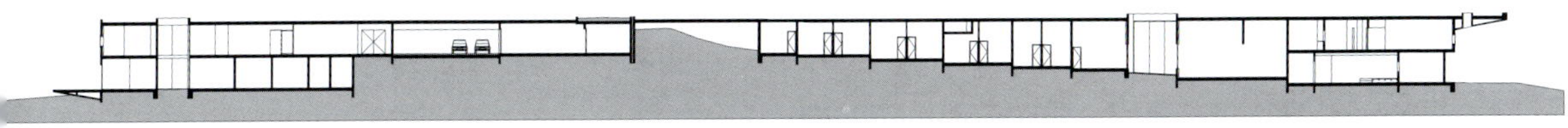

4

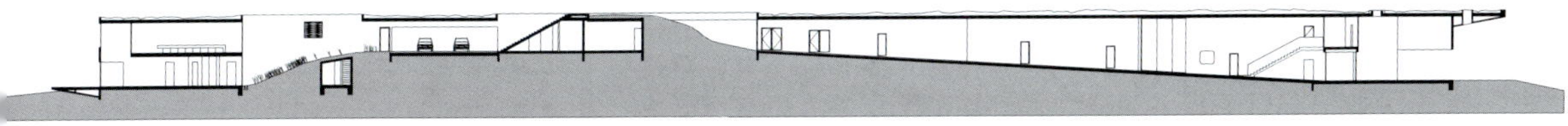

5

2

5

4

1

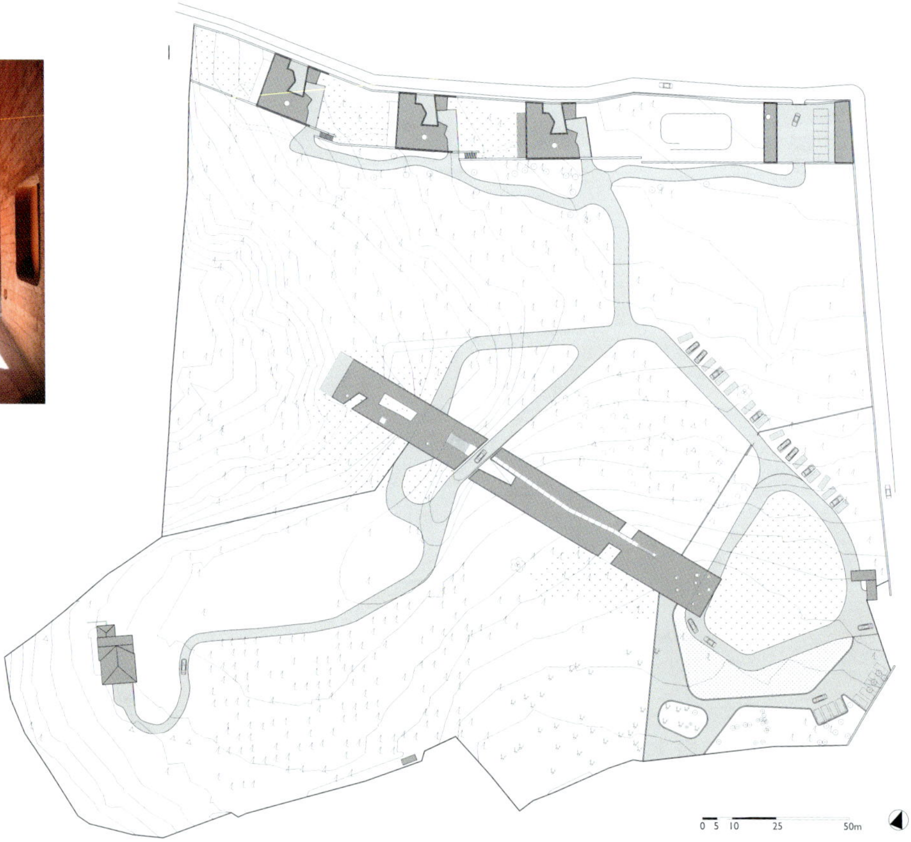

I situation of compound
2–3 chancellery entrance
4 chancellery corridor
5 chancellery

3

IX European Central Bank, Frankfurt am Main, Germany

The competition design for the head office of the European Central Bank (ECB) in Frankfurt covers 200,000 m^2 floor area on the site of the Grossmarkthalle beside the River Main. The ECB is a hub in a growing international financial network. The design for this building reflects this. It is not conceived as an autonomous object, but as an open, non-hierarchical system that forms part of a network. No fixed patterns of movement or communication have been laid down in the building. Instead, it offers room for a free and changing flow of people, data and material. The old Grossmarkthalle functions as a central point that provides access to this changeable network. Access roads and car parks that have been cut out of the surrounding land guarantee accessibility and security. The main traffic flows inside and outside the building are directed by vegetation.

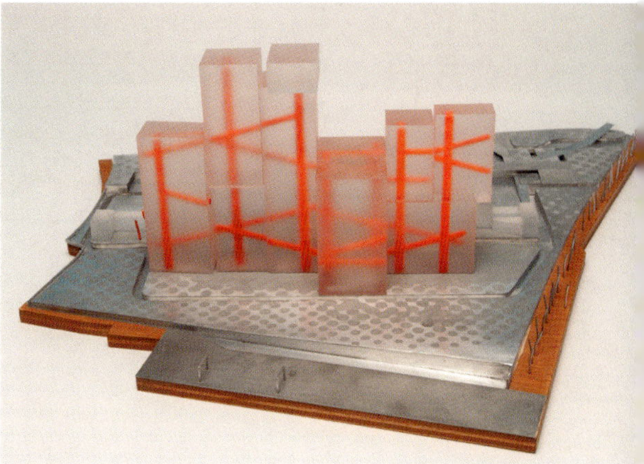

1

1 model of network

2 complex seen looking towards centre of Frankfurt

2

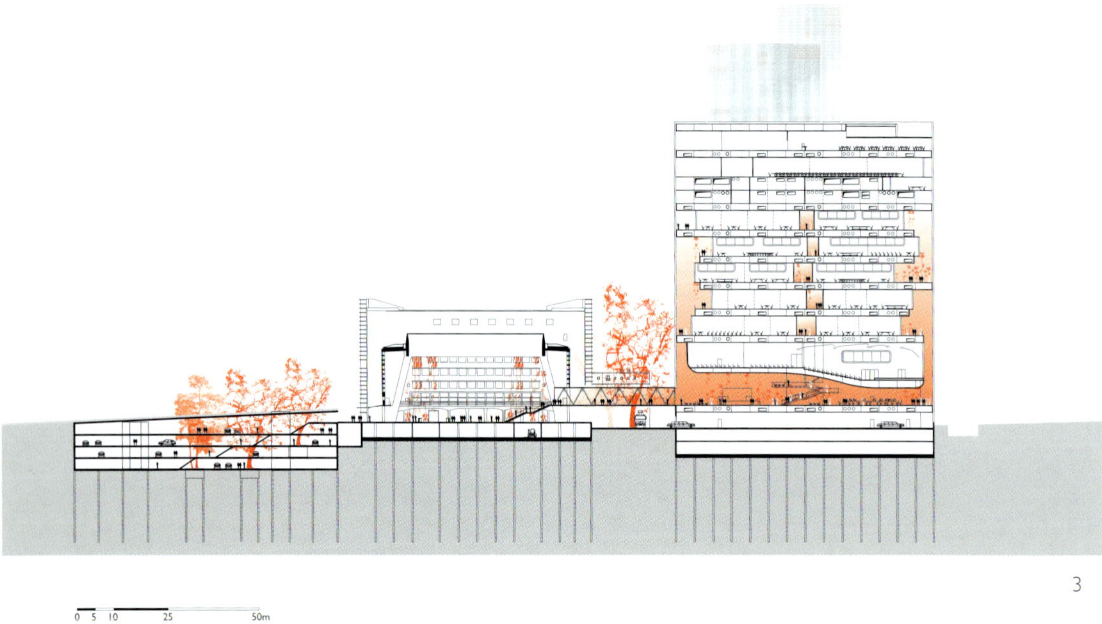

3

4

5

6

1 diagram of spatial organisation
2 first floor
3 transverse section
4 interior market hall
5 interior offices
6 interior congress tower block
7 sculpture garden between market hall and new building

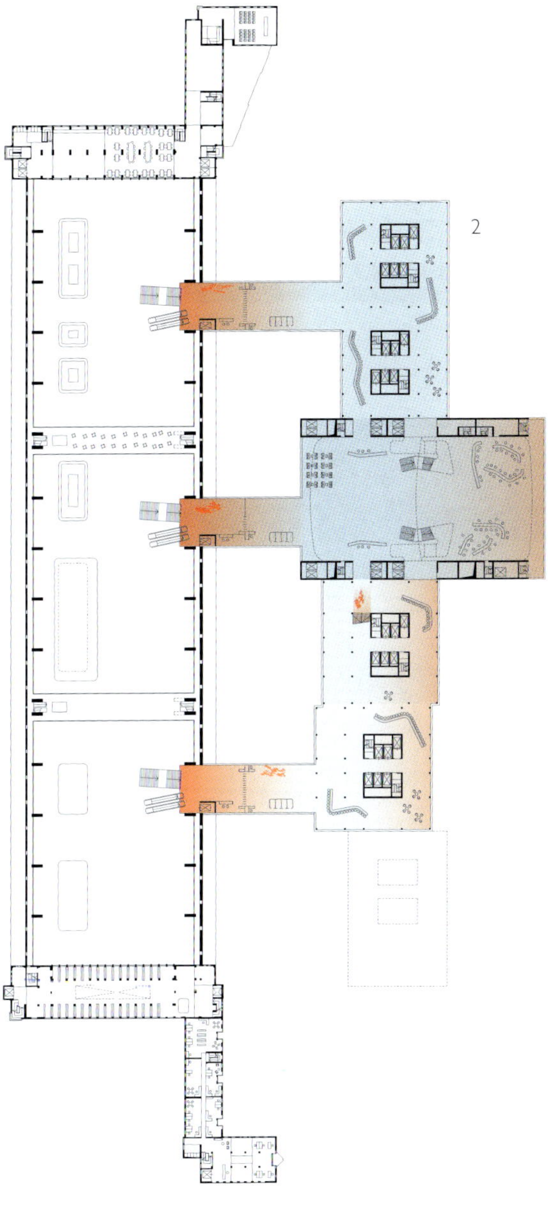

2

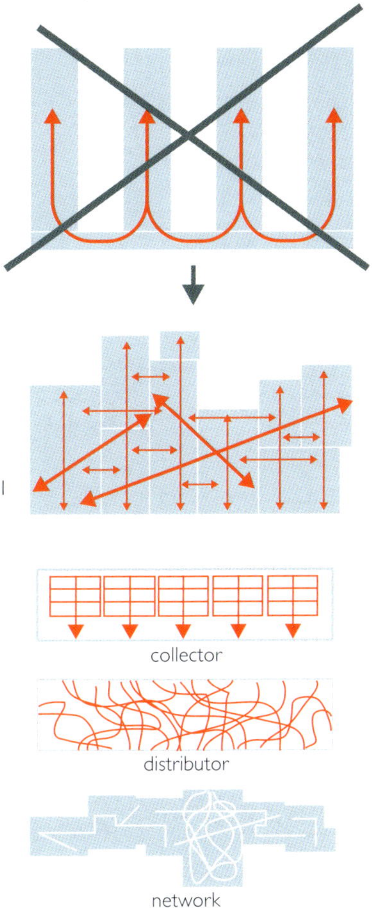

1

7

X AMOLF Institute for Atomic and Molecular Physics, Amsterdam

This laboratory for research in elementary physics is situated on the edge of Sciencepark Watergraafsmeer in East Amsterdam. It consists of three parallel components: a narrow office wing, a central volume with laboratories for experiments, and a section with workshops. The three components are separated by two inner corridors that physically isolate the vibration-sensitive laboratories from the other buildings. These 12-metre-high inner corridors make it possible to introduce large-scale equipment at any point to the stacked laboratories on either side. The central building is interrupted by a central hall that connects the two corridors, as well as connecting the two floors by means of large staircases. Walkways pass over the inner corridors to create circuits on the different levels.

5

6

3

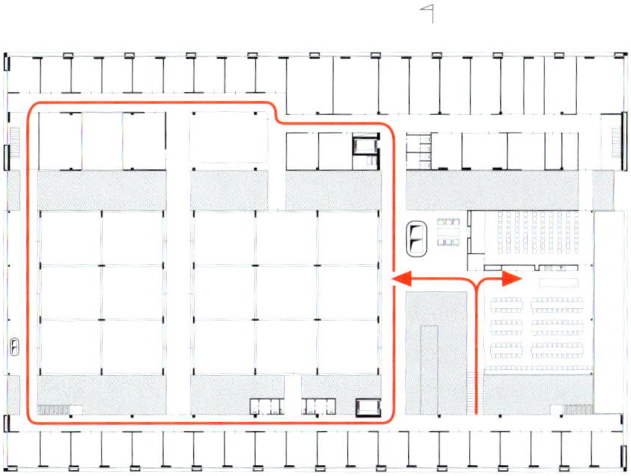

7

2

8

1

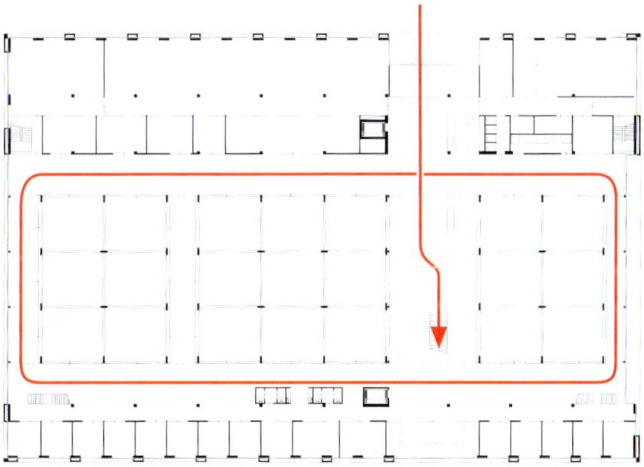

1 ground floor
2 first floor
3 second floor
4 transverse section
5 exterior
6 central hall from entrance
7 south corridor
8 foyer on second floor

4

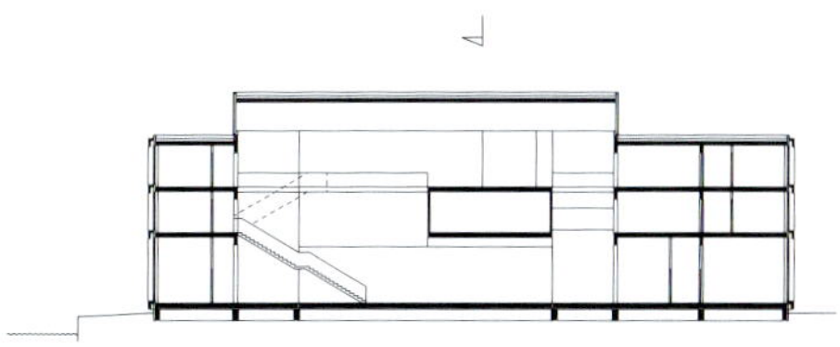

II Space in and around Buildings

Movement through a building can be used in the design as the basis for a clear coherence between spatiality and functionality. Similarly, the circulation can be used to structure the relation between a building and its immediate surroundings. Similar principles of connection and separation are operative here too, except that it is not the link between the circuit and the rooms that is primary, as it was with the corridor, but the link between public and private, outside and inside. The most obvious points for this are the ground floor and the ground level, but, as in the case of the corridor, the movement through the space can be horizontal or vertical.

Crucial for the connection and distinction between the building and its surroundings are the nuances and complexities that can arise when the distinction between inside and outside is not allowed to coincide exactly with that between public and private. The visual and actual accessibility of a building, the continuation of the inside outside and of the outside inside the building, touch on the same issues of privacy, diversity and density that arose in the previous chapter on the corridor.

A building whose relation with the city and the urban space has been designed in an unusual way is the **Trade Union Congress Memorial Building (TUC)** from 1956–1957, located in the heart of London close to the British Museum. The architect David du Rieu Aberdeen won the design competition for this building eight years earlier with a concept that is a combination of a trade union congress building with a war memorial. The courtyard, the roof of the sunken auditorium, contains a sculpture by Jacob Epstein on a base and socle in front of a high wall covered with green marble.

The TUC is built in a prewar Corbusian style. Thanks to the meticulous composition of the volumes and the use of a variety of durable materials (granite, bronze frames, ceramic tiles), the TUC, which has three walls facing the street, fits almost imperceptibly into its surroundings of big, closed neo-classical buildings. The ground floor is almost entirely transparent, a transparency that is perfectly in line with the democratic ideals of the trade union and affords a view from the street of the large courtyard with the war monument. Between the glass fronts and the street is a complex transitional zone in which stairways, ramps and landings make visible the movement to and inside the building. The most striking feature is the large semicircular staircase that emerges in the side street, between the entrance and exit of the underground car park. This zone can be interpreted as a twentieth-century version of the pavement zones of London in the eighteenth and nineteenth centuries, in which sunken intermediate areas with stairs separated the formal entrance from the entrance for domestics. The TUC building uses its transparency and strong sculpturality to call into question the distinction between inside and outside.

The same distinction is blurred even further in a building that was constructed at roughly the same time: the **Tokyo Metropolitan Festival Hall** (1957–1961). An earlier design by the architect Kunio Maekawa consisted of a number of pavilions linked by passages. When the available surface area was considerably reduced in size, he combined the several pavilions underneath a large roof, recalling traditional Japanese temple roofs. At ground level there is a far-reaching intertwining of the public space around the building and the parts of the building that are open to the public. The large foyer is accessible on various sides from the surrounding park. Adjoining the foyer are a number of outer areas that visually form a part of the park as gardens, but they are not accessible from the park. Dry ditches and retaining walls form a partition. The building is thus intrinsically connected with the park and contrasts sharply with the museum building opposite by Maekawa's mentor, Le Corbusier, which looks like a closed box that has just landed somewhere.

Linking large blocks of flats to the ground level often raises problems. Interesting solutions have been found in Chicago, the city where high-rise dwellings were invented. **Lake Point Tower** (1965) by Schipporeit-Heinrich Associates and Graham, Anderson, Probst and White, is connected with its surroundings in a remarkable way. From a distance, the colossal bronze-coloured glass tower looks like a meteorite that has crashed into a strip of land extending into Lake Michigan. In fact, the tower does not stand directly on the ground, but on a flat volume that fills the entire block and is as high as the surrounding harbour buildings. There are openings at ground level in the brickwork façades of this volume. The short side facing the city has an opening leading to the commercial area behind. On the south side there is a large opening in front of a semicircular forecourt that is partly roofed. Drivers and pedestrians can enter this area to reach the lobby or the car park. This forecourt connects the tower block with the public space in a spectacular way; the circular opening affords a dizzying vista of the sixty-storey tower block. Besides commercial areas and a car park, the box also contains shared facilities: the roof houses a large garden with a swimming pool and ponds.

A closer connection with the public space can be achieved by directing a route that is open to the public through a building. The **Ford Foundation Building** (1963–1968) in midtown Manhattan by Kevin Roche and John Dinkeloo is a prototypical example of this. The Ford Foundation is a robust cube between 42nd and 43rd Street. The northern and western sides of the volume contain twelve storeys of offices; the rest of the space is a large atrium intersected by a path that links the

TUC Memorial Building, London, UK
David du Rieu Aberdeen and Partners
1956–1957

1
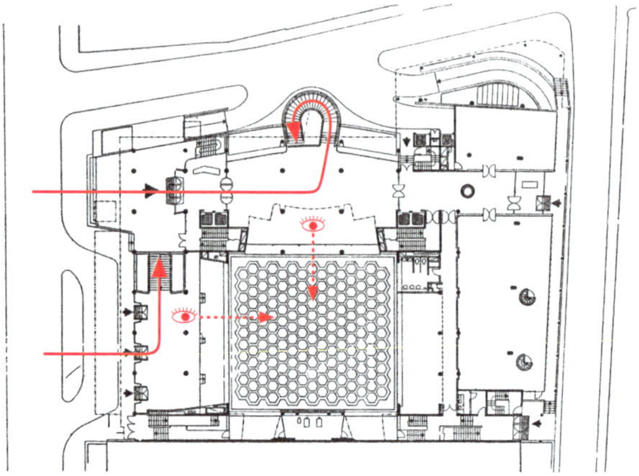

5

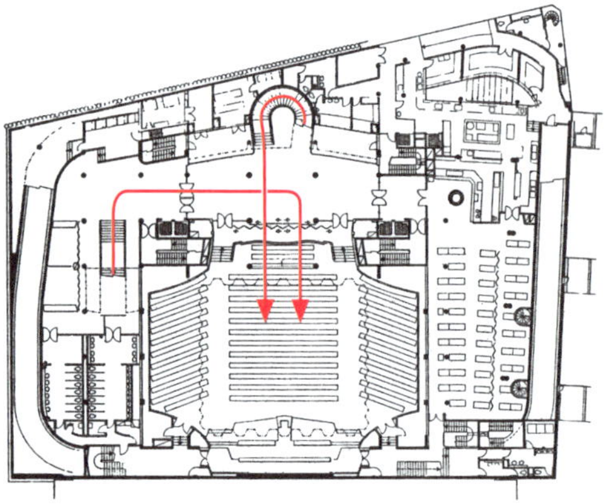
2

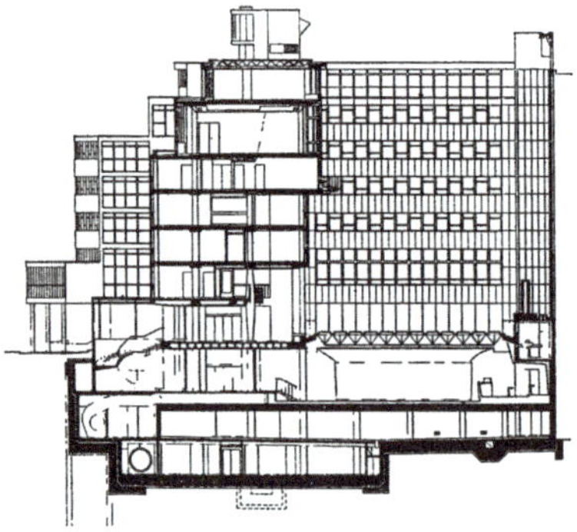
4

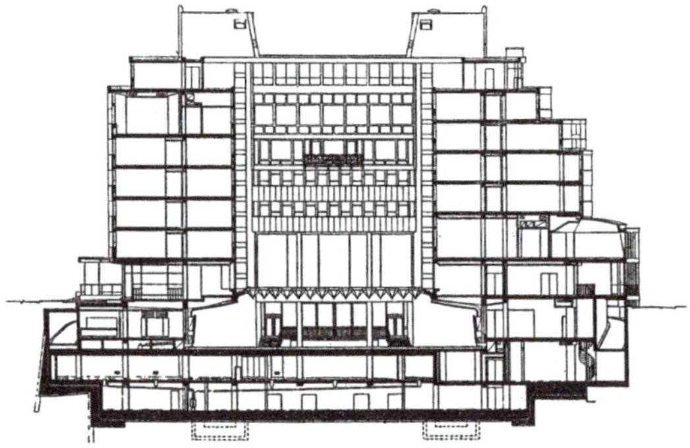
3

0 2 5 10 25m

8

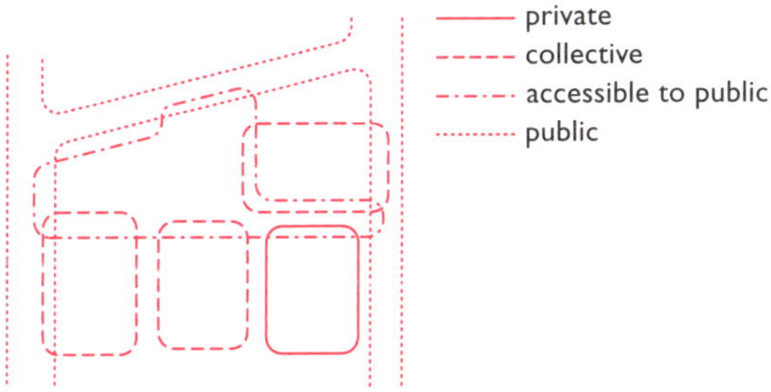

7 

6 

1 ground floor
2 basement
3–4 cross-sections
5 side façade with staircase between entrance hall and congress hall
6 stairs to parking garage near main entrance
7 interior of hall between street and inner courtyard
8 separate entrance for congress hall

Tokyo Metropolitan Festival Hall, Tokyo, Japan
Kunio Maekawa
1957–1961

6

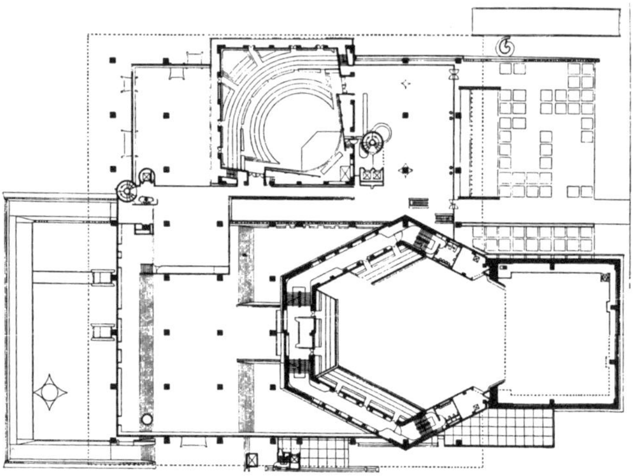

2

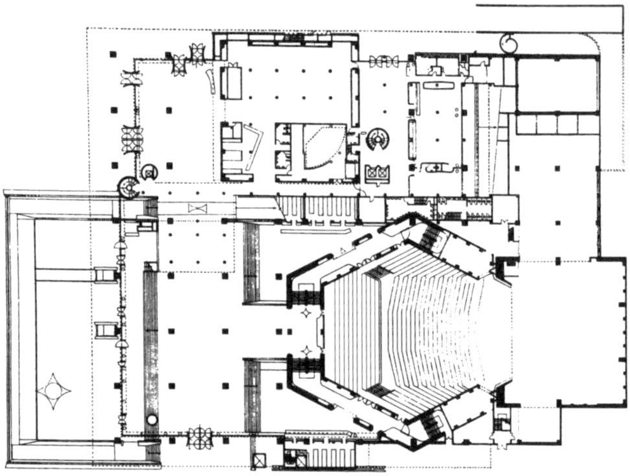

1

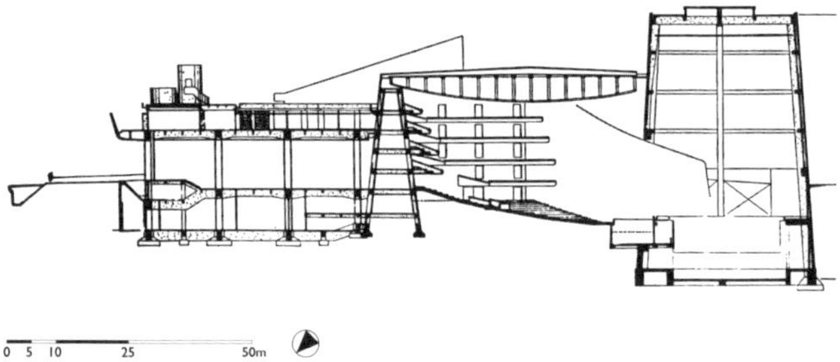

3

4

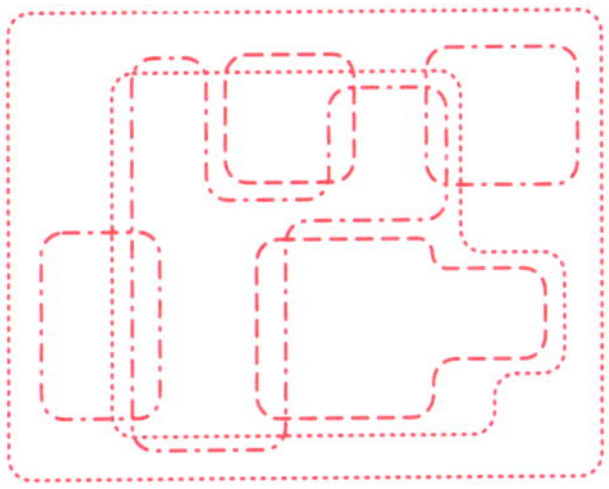

5

7

1 ground floor
2 first floor
3 cross-section main auditorium
4–5 façades of foyers with terraces
6 foyer
7 main auditorium

Lake Point Tower, Chicago, Illinois, US

Schipporeit–Heinrich Associates

1965

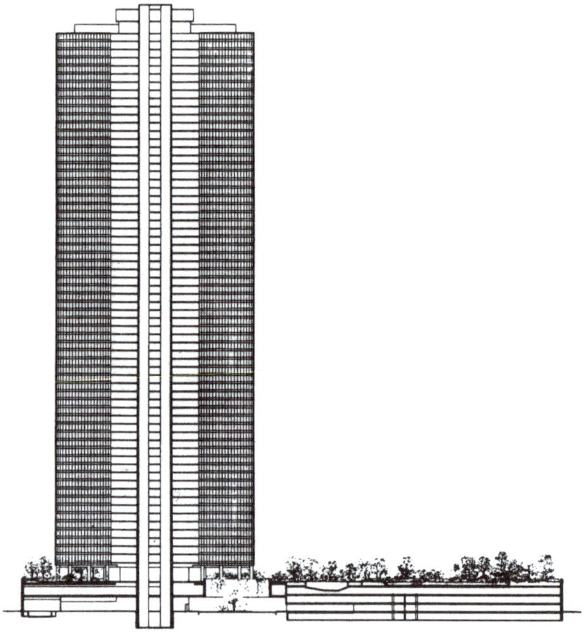

4

8

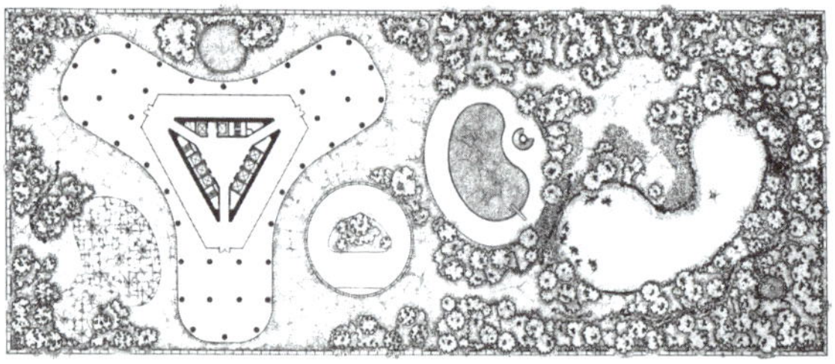

2

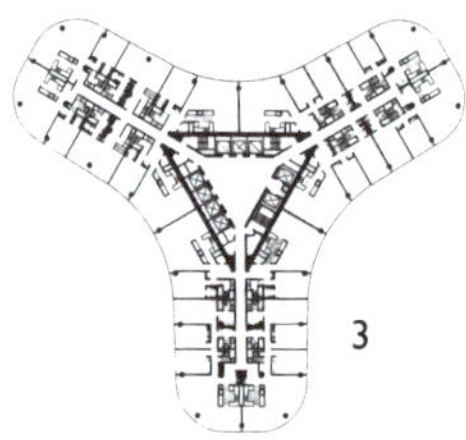

3

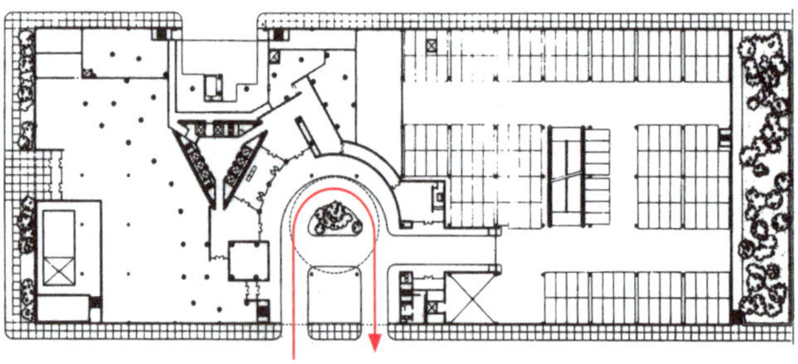

1

5

6

7

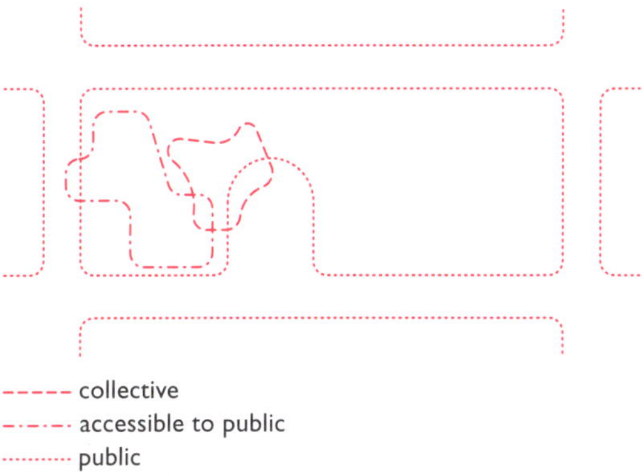

1 ground floor
2 roof garden
3 apartments in tower block
4 cross-section with forecourt
5–6 aerial view
7 forecourt
8 view of tower from forecourt

The Ford Foundation Building, New York, US

Kevin Roche, John Dinkeloo and Associates

1963–1968

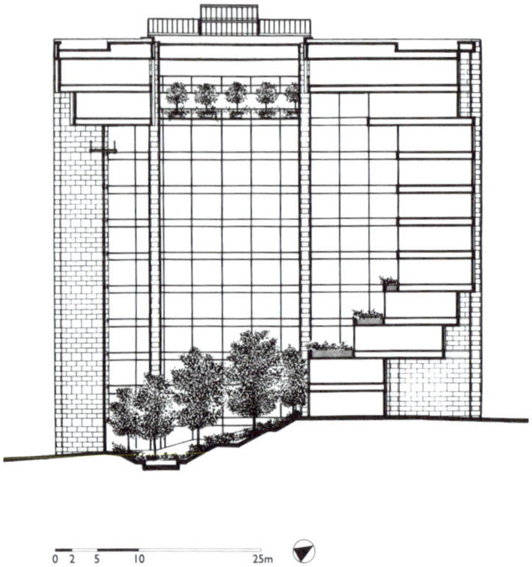

2

3

4

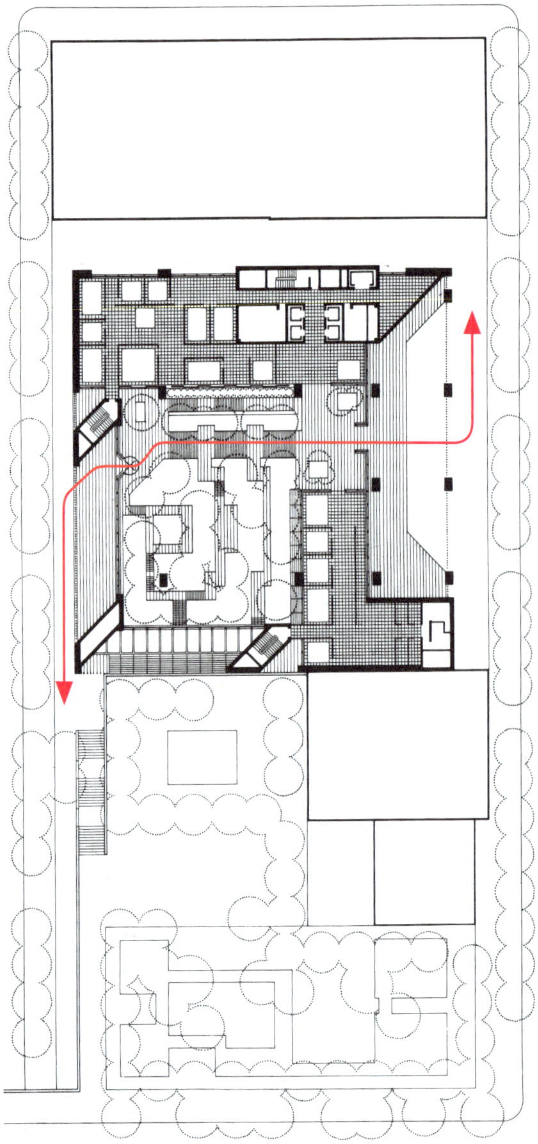

1

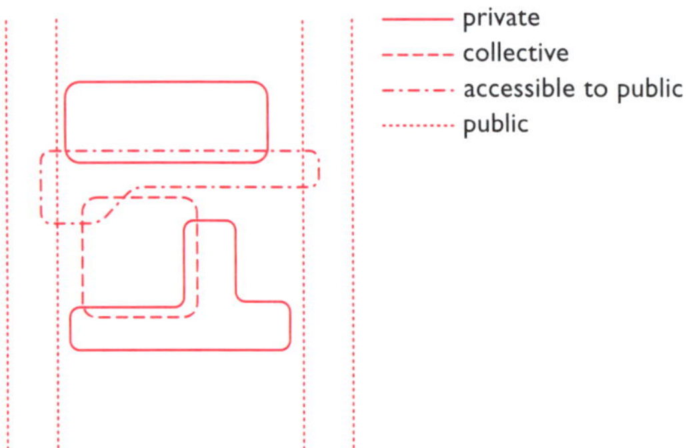

1 ground level
2 cross-section
3–4 atrium

two streets with one another. The path contains a number of large steps to bridge the difference in gradient between the streets. The inner walls of the atrium form a neutral background for the vegetation, which follows the slope before growing upwards over a number of terraces.

The public route through the **Neue Staatsgalerie** in Stuttgart (1977) by James Stirling is more complex than in the Ford Foundation. The appearance of this museum building is characterised by a large number of quotations from the history of architecture. Ironically enough, this causes the architecture of this building to look dated rather than timeless. Stirling's penchant for citations also diverts attention from the brilliant way in which he solved the spatial puzzle.

The museum is built on a slope. The difference in level made it possible to allow the route that goes straight through the museum to link the front with the rear to intersect with the internal routes of the museum without any conflicts. Although the public space is organised along the central axis of the symmetrical museum building, the route only coincides with that axis at a few points.

The route leads upwards over a series of ramps that connect a number of terraces on the slope through a gateway to the open rotunda in the middle of the complex. Visitors who reach this spot have the idea that they are in the museum itself, but the works of art remain inaccessible. The route continues upwards along the wall of the rotunda and intersects the roofs of the museum rooms. The route ends at the services building, a separate volume on the same scale as the other buildings along the street at the rear. There is a major contrast between the monumental start of the route and the almost nonchalant end in the street at the rear. This contrast underlines the fact that the importance of this route lies not in connecting the two parts of the city between which the building is situated, but in establishing a subtle link between the public space and the museum.

Public routes through buildings make the architecture subservient to the city, since the space that is taken over by the building is compensated by new public routes. An example of this that is much clearer than Stirling's museum is the complex for **The Economist** in London (1959–1964). At the end of a closed block, Alison and Peter Smithson designed three buildings with different functions: an office tower block, a bank, and a block of flats. The three buildings follow the building line of the block and combine with the adjoining Boodle's Club to form the corner points of an open intermediate space that is linked with the neighbouring streets. This intermediate space is slightly raised, and mediates between the different street levels on both sides of the complex.

In The Economist building, the new public space is a means of achieving density. The sixteen-storey office block towers way above the surrounding buildings. The Economist adds public space to the city without disturbing the continuity of the

Neue Staatsgalerie, Stuttgart, Germany

James Stirling

1977–1984

6

1

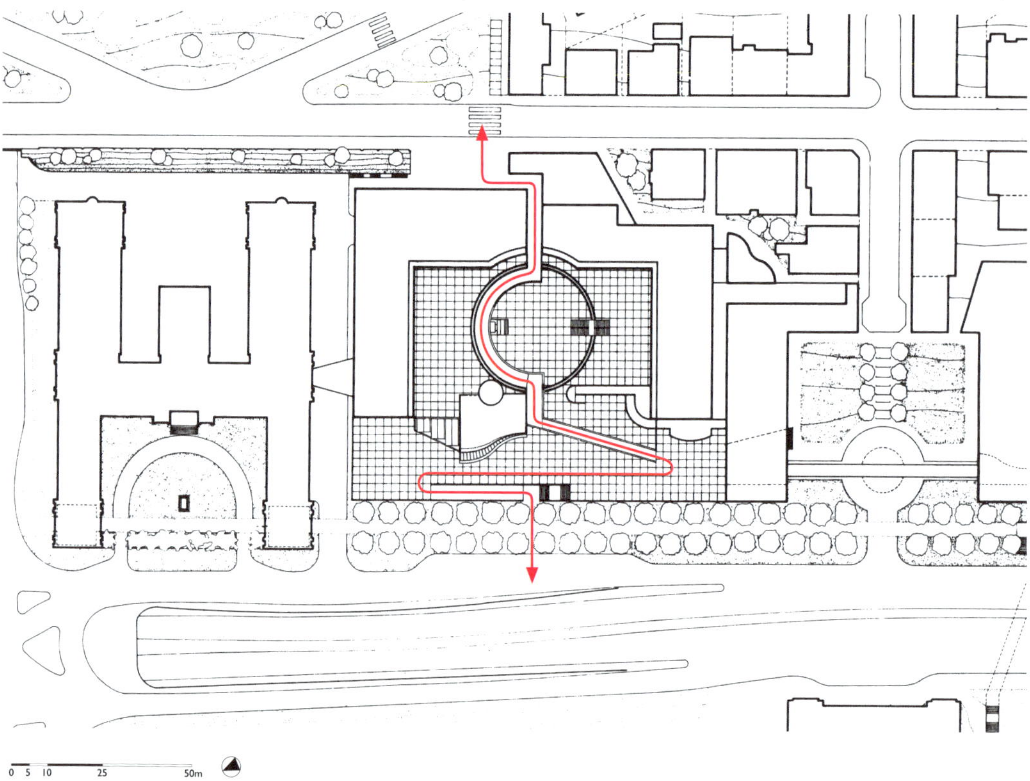

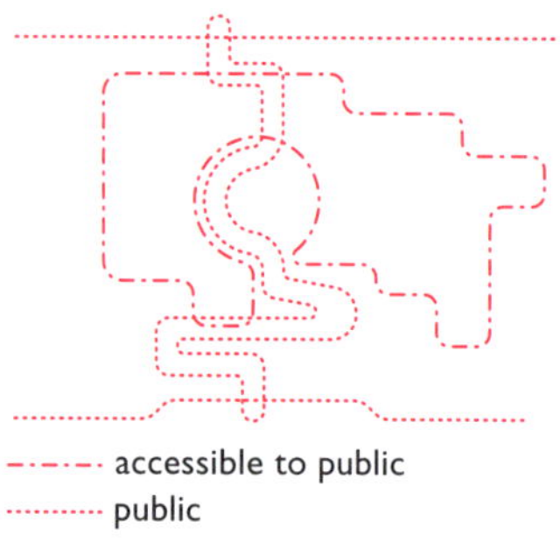

4

5

2

3

1 building at level of the outdoor areas
2–3 front of building with ramps
4 rotunda seen from museum
5 route intersects building
6 route at rear

The Economist Building, St. James's Street, London, UK

Alison and Peter Smithson

1959–1964

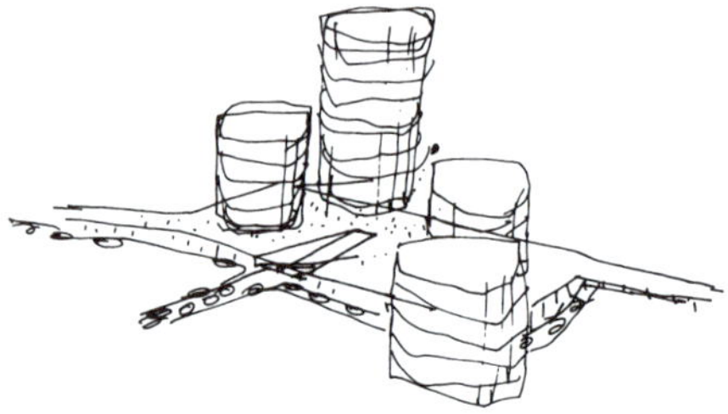

4

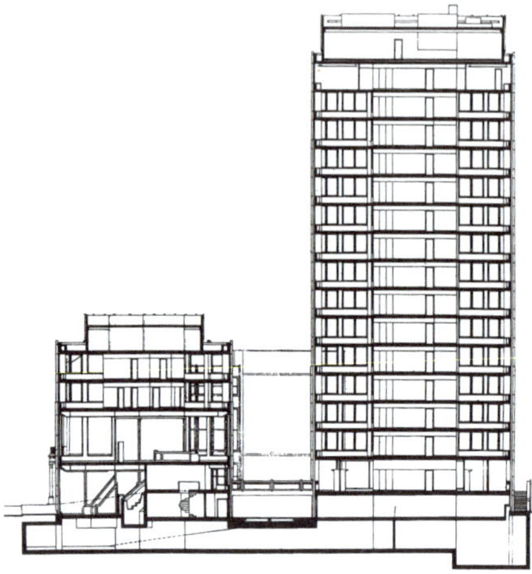

3

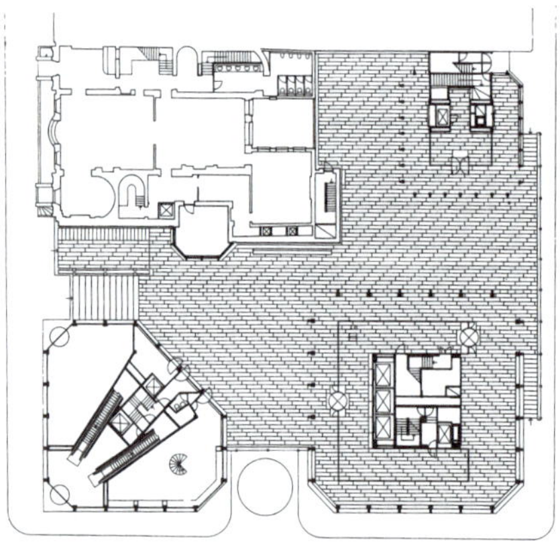

1

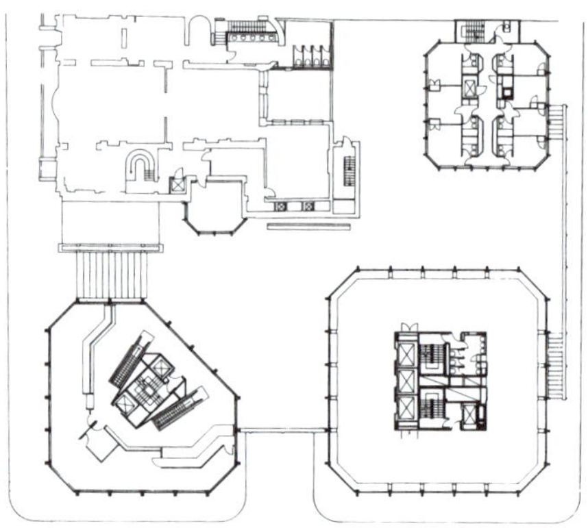

2

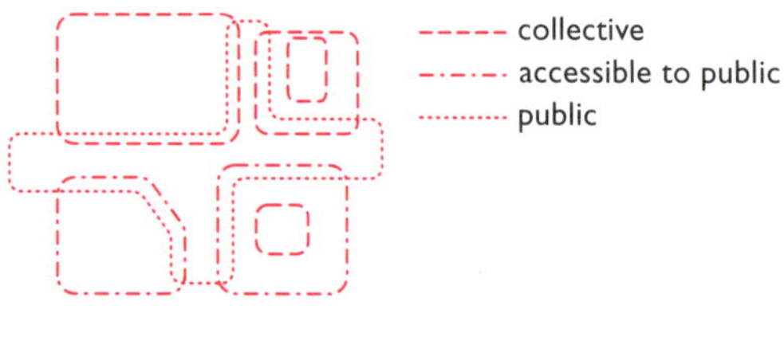

5

7

8

6

1 ground level and square level
2 first floor
3 cross-section of bank and offices
4 sketch for an urban complex
5 aerial view
6–8 the intermediate space

street, but by establishing new links. In this respect the complex differs from the way in which public space was added to cities in the US during the same period by designing plazas in front of buildings. One of the most famous examples of this is Mies van der Rohe's Seagram Building. These plazas are virtually autonomous spaces in spatial terms, and they break up the block structure of the grid city. In the case of The Economist, the space around the buildings is not autonomous, but forms a part of the street areas surrounding the complex. Sketches and photomontages indicate that the designers viewed The Economist as a prototypical fragment of the separation of pedestrians and car traffic. Such a separation of traffic might work on a large scale (although there are countless examples from the 1960s and 1970s in which raising the pedestrian level has led to unfortunate and only moderately functional solutions), but The Economist is too small for that. Still, as a monumental empty space among the crowded streets of London, this raised area does provide a welcome relief.

Another project in which the introduction of new intermediate spaces has enabled a densification of the building is Luigi Moretti's complex beside the **Corso Italia** in the centre of Milan (1949–1956). The sculptural complex, which replaces a destroyed part of a block, contains shops, offices and apartments. It consists of several volumes that are precisely aligned with the existing buildings and the original building lines. Slightly setting back the building line beside the Corso where several streets intersect has produced a small square. A sharp overhang six metres above the pavement still indicates the building line. This overhang is the pointed tip of a highly articulated volume that balances on a lower section like a battleship.

The main intervention is to the right of this battleship: a partly roofed street has been created at right angles to the Corso Italia which makes the tall volume behind it on the plot both visible and accessible. An enormous incision that divides the top seven storeys of this volume into two marks this new street, which continues beneath the building on columns to the gardens behind the building. Ramps left and right lead down to the car park, thereby detaching the large volume even more from the ground level. The formal and functional complexity of Moretti's building is not an isolated phenomenon, but is closely connected with the desire to turn it into a network that adds space and activity to the city.

An unusual example of the building as an urban network is the **Bank of England** complex, which was created between 1788 and 1833 as the result of a series of renovations and renewals designed by John Soane. Apart from the outside façade, all of these interventions and additions were replaced around 1920 by a less complex new building.

Soane's Bank occupied an entire block in the City of London. It comprised a labyrinthine complex of buildings, linked by corridors and courtyards. This laby-

Corso Italia, Milan, Italy
Luigi Moretti
1949–1956

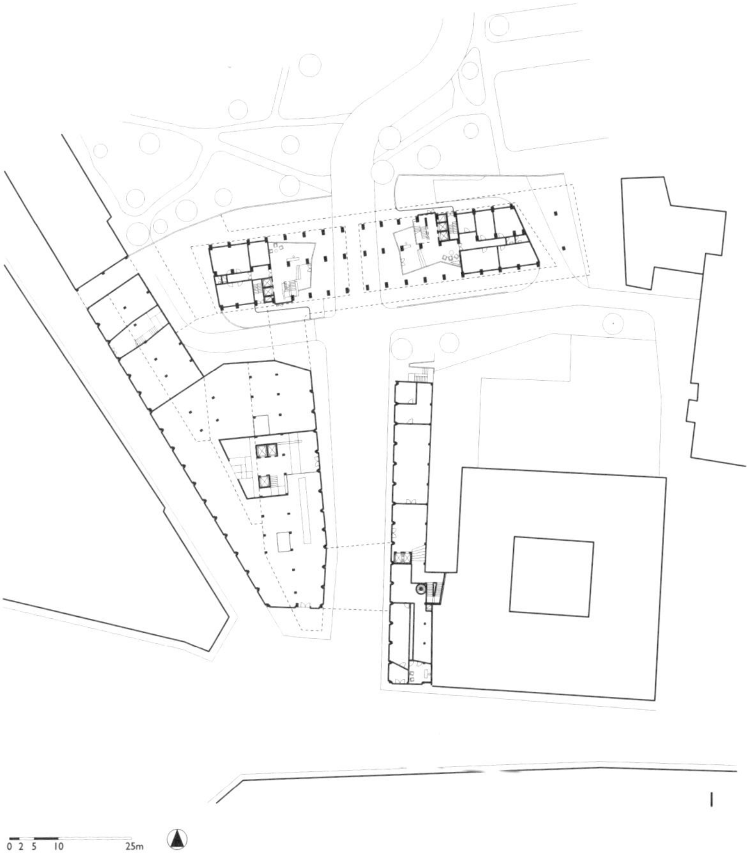

1

2

3

5

4

1 ground level
2–3 sketches of preliminary design
4 street at right angles to Corso Italia
5 rear of complex

rinth of fragments was held together by a continuous outer wall. Four gateways, one in each street wall, gave access to a system of connections that pervaded the entire building. The passages and courtyards had an unprecedented complexity, deliberately designed by Soane to afford persons traversing them a constantly changing array of spaces and light.

As the national bank, the building had to radiate the solidity of an impregnable fortress, but behind the closed walls was an open structure in which the city's network of streets and squares was continued.

The principle of viewing buildings not as isolated elements, but as spatial and functional parts of a larger whole, was elaborated in different ways in two large-scale housing complexes from the 1920s and 1950s: **Rabenhof** in Vienna, and **Conjunto Juscelino Kubitschek** in Belo Horizonte. In these complexes, a large degree of differentiation has been achieved in the intertwining of the building and public space because besides public outdoor spaces there are also collective ones.

The Conjunto Juscelino Kubitschek in Belo Horizonte (1951), a plan by Oscar Niemeyer, extends over two blocks in the characteristic diagonal grid of Belo Horizonte: a regular square block, and an irregular, smaller block, situated at one of the large intersections. Initially the idea was to include a large number of commercial and cultural facilities in the complex as well as offices and apartments, but the final result was a simpler programme.

The articulation here is organised vertically. By making use of the difference in gradient, Niemeyer has designed three ground levels on top of one another, each of which is connected with the city around it.

The lowest ground level is directly adjacent to the square and contains shops in a number of freely formed clusters. The clusters are roofed by an enormous surface that resumes the contour of the block. This roof is a large collective outdoor area for the apartments. The form that was implemented has vegetation and tennis courts, but the programme was much more extensive in the original design.

The entrance hall to the building is also situated at this level. The roof of this entrance forms the third level, which is public and consists of a square offering a view of the city over the collective outdoor area.

Rabenhof (1928–1930) by the architects Heinrich Schmid and Hermann Aichinger, is one of the famous superblocks of Vienna. The complex contains 1,100 apartments, 38 shops, and a large number of collective facilities. The plan differs from many other blocks, such as the Karl-Marx-hof by Karl Ehn, because it is not an isolated complex, but carries over into the existing buildings and road patterns. Rabenhof's blocks closely follow the existing building lines, but gradually change shape to form a successive series of public and collective areas. The distinction

The Bank of England, London, UK

John Soane

1788–1833

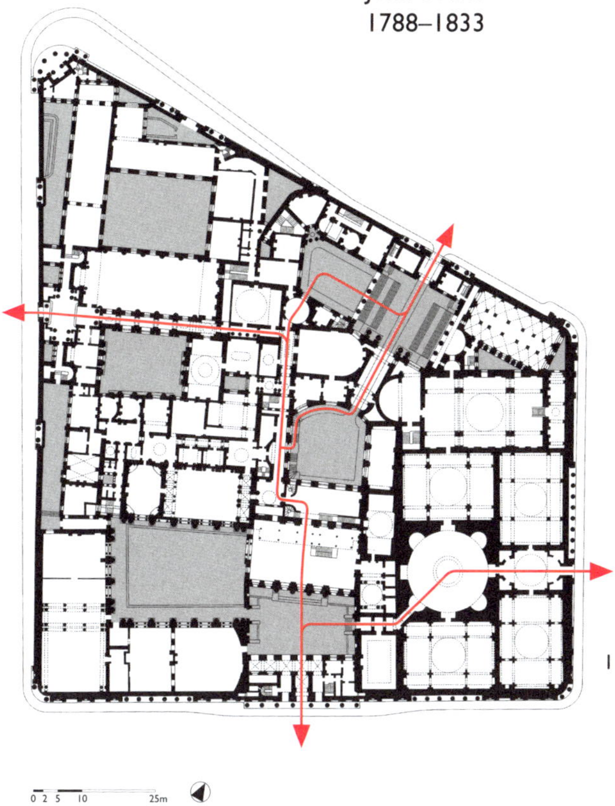

1

4

5

3

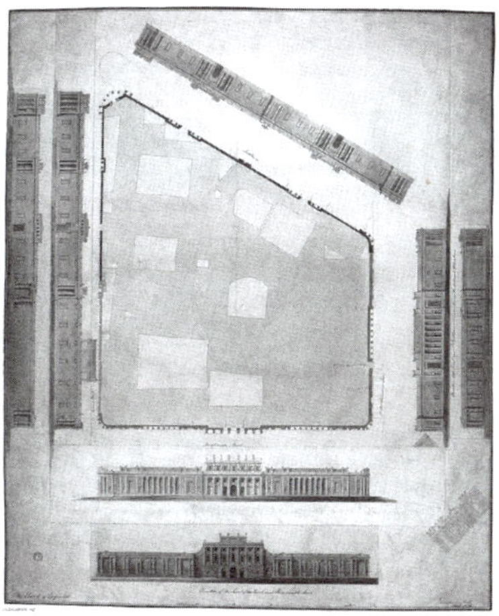

2

1 ground floor
2 mass and street façades
3 bird's-eye view
4 view of two inner courtyards
5 interior circa 1920

Rabenhof, Vienna, Austria

Heinrich Schmid; Hermann Aichinger

1928–1930

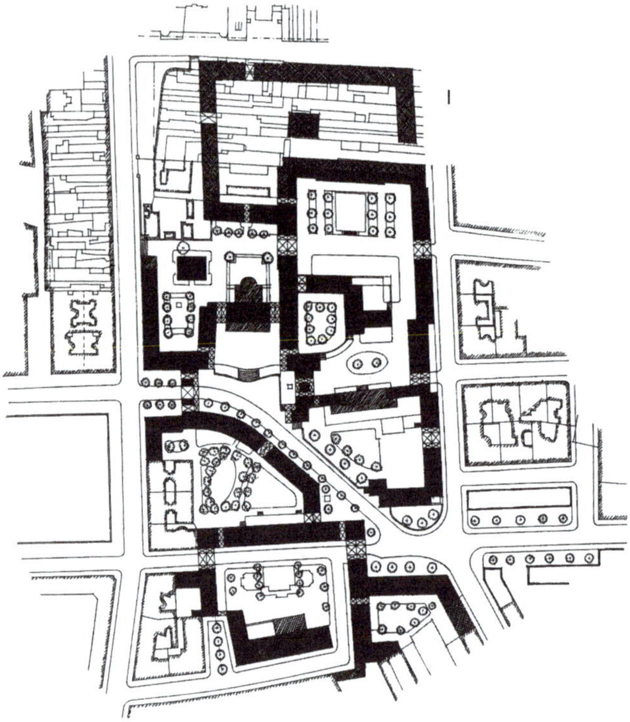

1

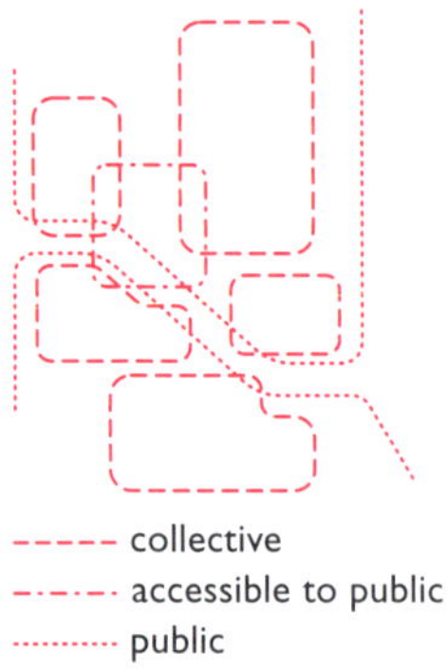

3

2

1 block at ground level
2–3 streets intersect the courtyards

Juscelino Kubitschek Complex, Belo Horizonte, Brazil
Oscar Niemeyer
1951

1
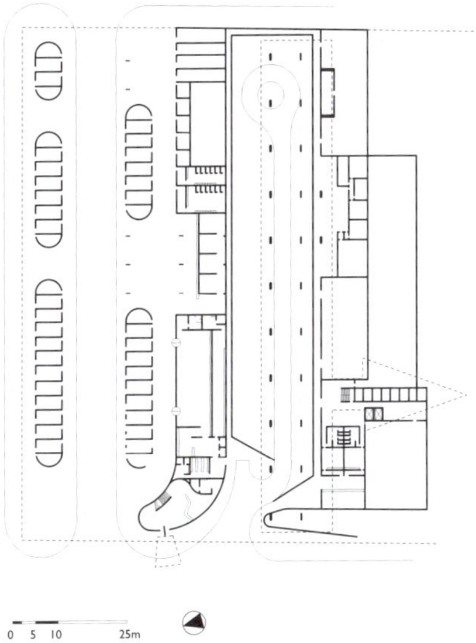

2
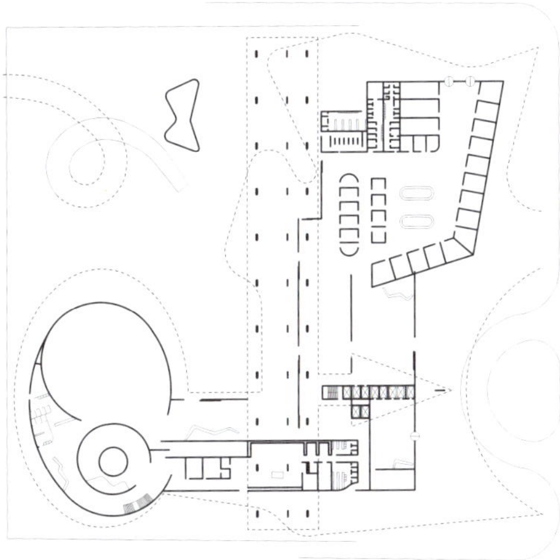

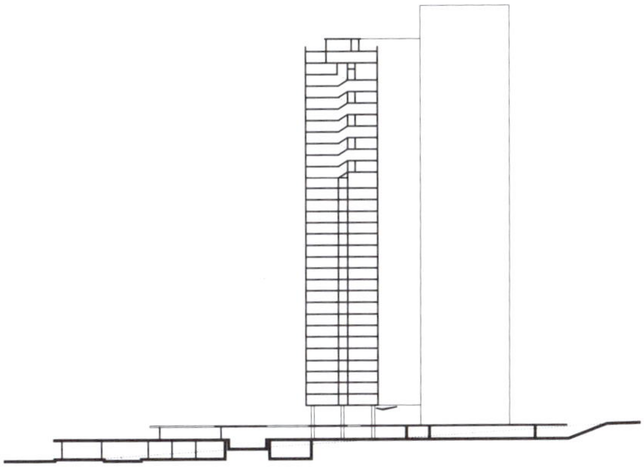

3

4
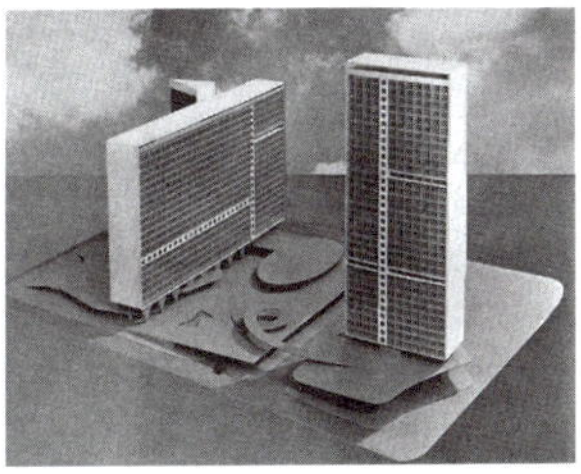

5

1 ground level with shops
2 first roof level with collective facilities
3 cross-section
4 scale model
5 implemented complex

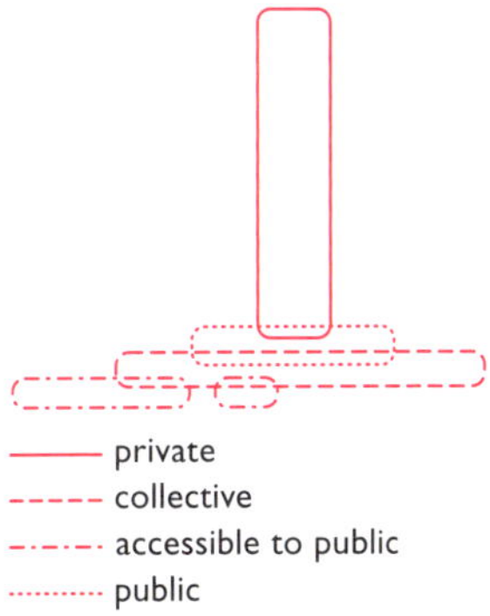

between street and courtyard is thereby abolished: all of the space is part of a continuous network that, in spite of the large scale of the new buildings, brings differentiation and articulation to the city.

Rabenhof resembles the network of the **Inns of Court** in London, which display a particularly successful example of the intertwining of public space and building, and of collective and public areas. The Inns of Court, which developed between the fourteenth and the twentieth century, mark the transition from the City of London to the City of Westminster. They consist of a number of complexes of buildings with a typology virtually identical to the colleges of Oxford and Cambridge, but which in this case accommodate members of the legal profession. The Inns are situated in an almost uninterrupted series, concealed behind the buildings that line the city streets with a predominantly east-west orientation. The buildings of the Inns are grouped around internal streets, squares and gardens, making it possible to reconcile diverse programmes with one another in a high density.

The streets and squares of the Inns are directly connected to the city around them, but they can be closed off from it. These closable public areas in turn contain closable collective areas: in many cases the green lawns in the Inns are fenced off and are only open to the public for a part of the day at most. The route from Gray's Inn in the north to the bank of the Thames in the south comprises a diverse and changing series of spaces, although at many points one has to turn a blind eye to the mass of (often very expensive) lawyers' cars parked there in order to appreciate the variety of spatial nuances to the full.

The Inns of Court, London, UK
14th century

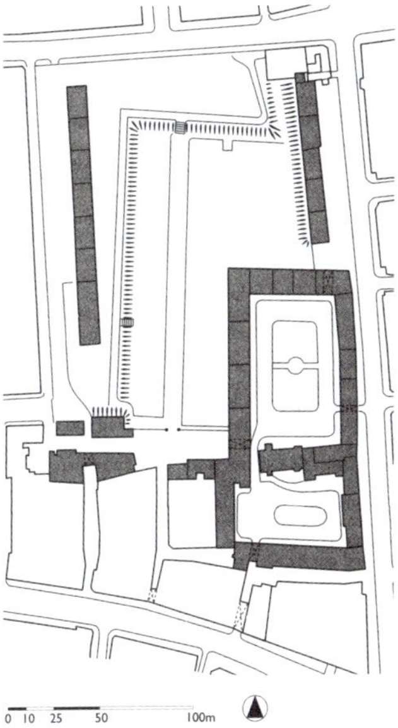

2

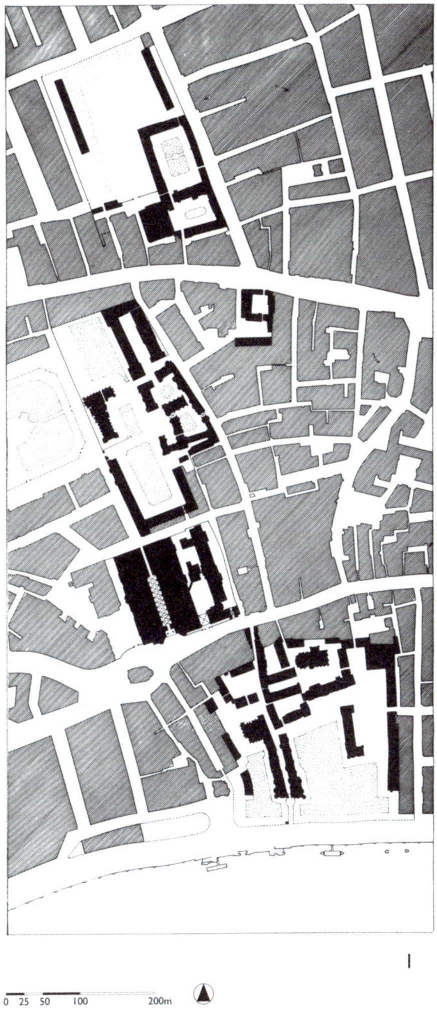

1

3

4

5

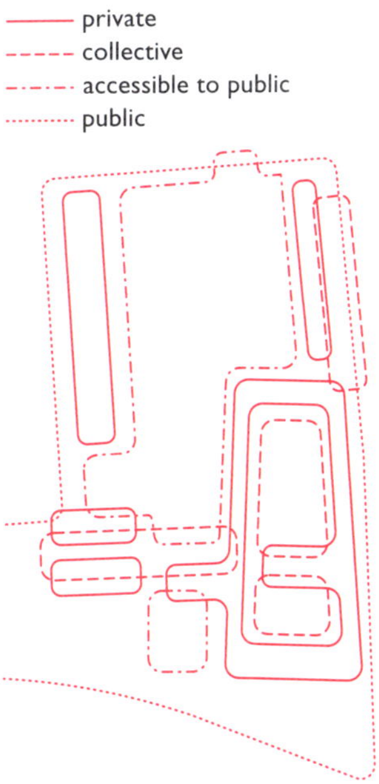

1 The Inns, from top to bottom:
Gray's Inn, Staple Inn, Lincoln's Inn, Law Courts, The Temple
2 Gray's Inn
3 Lincoln's Inn, the Stone Buildings
4 Gray's Inn, the Walks
5 Temple, the Middle Temple Hall

A building that is not linked to its surroundings is an obstacle. That is why areas that establish a link between a building and its surroundings are essential. Public areas, areas that are open to the public, or collective areas that are carved out of the building mass can enhance the interface between the building and its surroundings and prevent the city from being reduced to uniform public space and equally uniform closed building masses. Besides forming a spatial link between the building and its surroundings, such transitional areas and intermediate spaces can absorb different (potentially conflicting) functions and enable higher building densities. The connecting area organises the relation between the building and the city, just as the space for circulation regulates the relation between the areas inside a building.

The connecting area may assume a variety of guises. In the apartment blocks in Emmen, on IJburg in Amsterdam, and in Houtrust in The Hague, collective open spaces establish a link between home and public space. In the apartments in Moerwijk (The Hague), Huizen, and the Oostoever in Amsterdam, the collective intermediate space is part of a more complex transition from public to private; it makes the buildings accessible without disturbing the privacy of the residents. In the residential care centre in Diemen, the big linear hall with adjacent terraces and patios functions as a mediator between the different departments and services in the building, on the one hand, and between the building and its setting, on the other. The Laakhaven office and apartment complex in The Hague has a virtually entirely open ground floor level. It contains a variety of public spaces and areas that are open to the public, which regulates the accessibility of the complex itself and the surrounding area.

R R R R R

R R R R R

R R R R R

R R R R R

R R R R R

1 Office and apartment complex, Laakhaven, The Hague

The Laakhaven complex, bordered by the Waldorpstraat and the Leeghwaterkade, is characterised by a combination of functions. It comprises 30,000 m² of office space, forty apartments, and a number of commercial areas. The complex is framed by a glass envelope, which indicates the limits of the maximal building envelope as laid down in the master plan for this location. The different functions are placed inside this envelope as separate objects. The offices are accommodated in blocks that vary in height, orientation and façade materials. The two apartment blocks in the complex are orientated towards the water of the Laakhaven. The terraces of the apartments extend outside the glass envelope. All the building volumes are raised above ground level, leaving it free for a number of public and collective functions: a public passage, an atrium that is open to the public, shops, and collective facilities for the offices here, such as business restaurants. This results in a spectrum of relations between the building and its surroundings at street level.

3

2

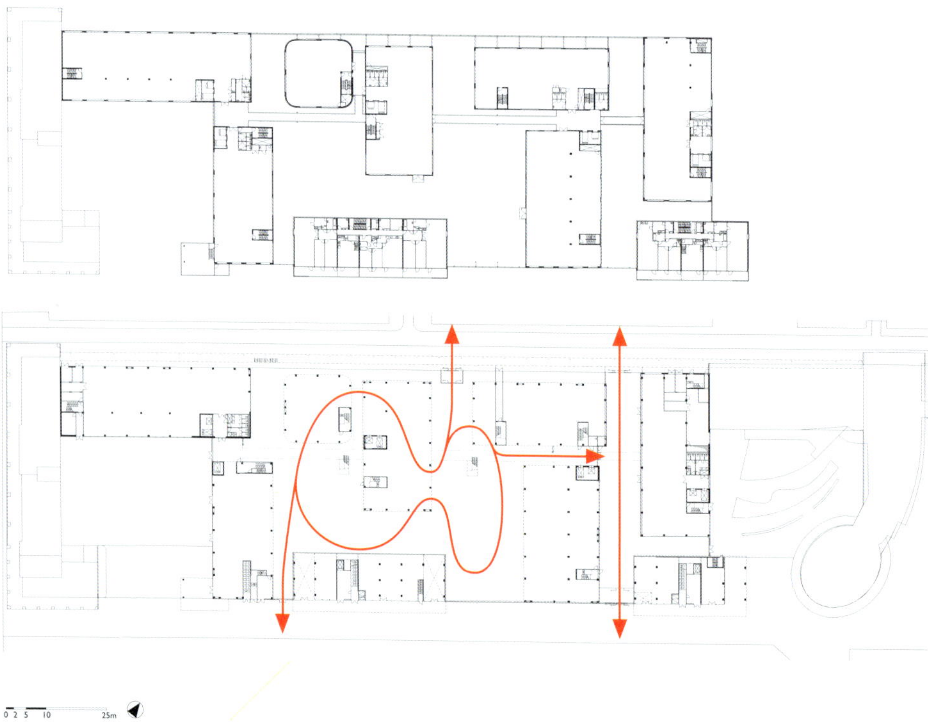

1

4

1 ground floor
2 second floor
3 aerial view
4 south elevation
5 passage

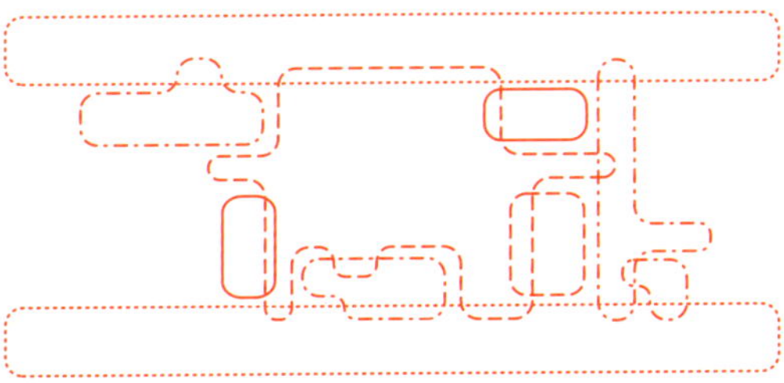

private
collective
accessible to public
public

5

2

1 volumes in envelope
2–4 atrium areas

3

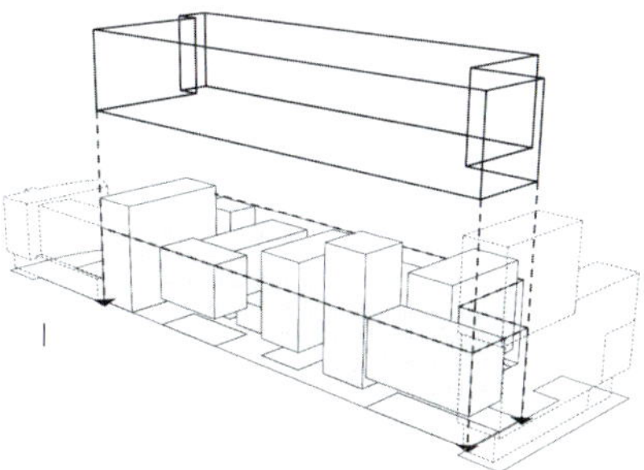

1

4

11 Marktplein apartment block, Emmen

The building brings order to the heterogeneous combination of the leafy village square of Emmen, the Hondsrugweg with a high noise level, and the dreary car parks on the north side. It is a highly articulated volume that unites the different building heights in the area. The curved lower part of the building follows the obligatory 'historical' building line, while the apartments above it follow the noise contour. The apartments are orientated towards the south and west for the sun and the view. Large terraces and verandas form a screen between the apartments and the traffic noise. The top two storeys contain very large apartments. The connecting space at ground level is a forecourt, shielded from the street by a wall, which forms a green buffer between the block and the city.

4

1

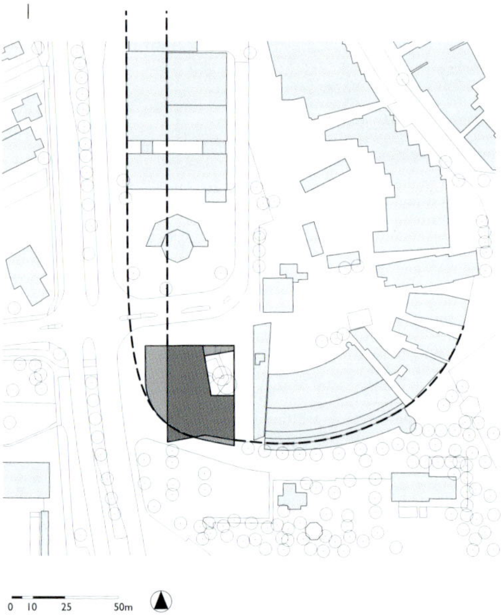

5

1 situation
2 ground level with forecourt
3 apartment level
4–5 seen from Marktplein
6–7 forecourt
8 entrance hall

6

8

7

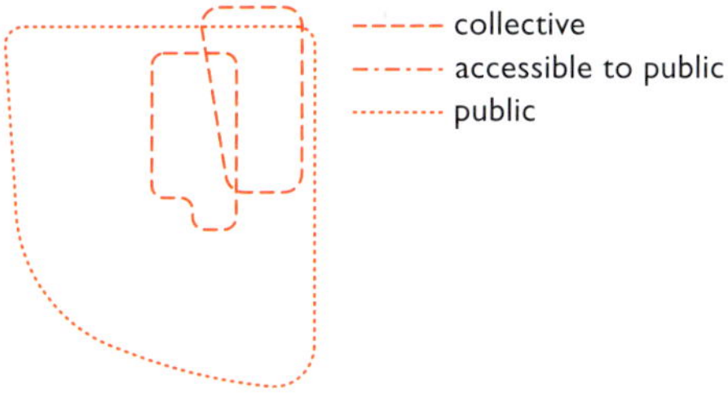

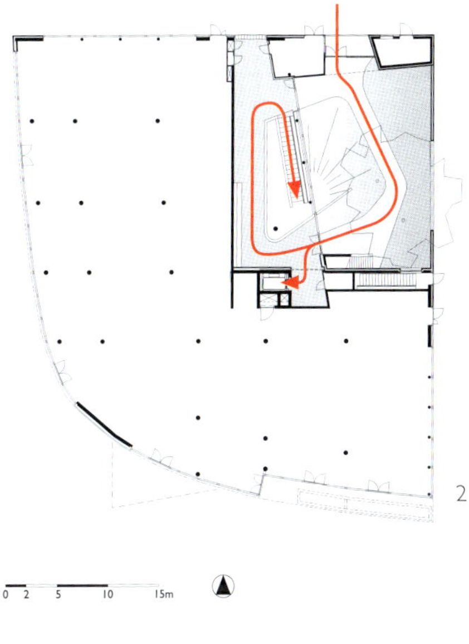

2

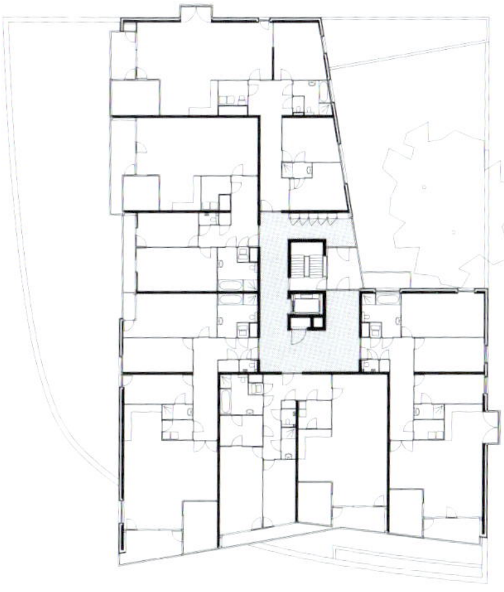

3

III Apartment block 23B1, IJburg, Amsterdam

The block, which is intersected by a canal, consists of three different buildings, each with a hybrid form. Each hybrid contains high-rise apartments (eight storeys) and low-rise homes (three-storeys), with a smooth transition between the two types. Each hybrid owes its characteristic form to the silhouette of the high-rise block. Block 23B1 has 26 low-rise homes and 52 high-rise apartments, a commercial area, and a semi-sunken underground car park. The precisely stipulated building envelope, in combination with the programme, requires a double line of buildings on top of the ground area. An inner street has been cut out of the mass for this purpose. This inner street intersects the block in different ways and leads to a diversity of types of homes and apartments. With respect to the low-rise homes, it runs between two rows, one on either side of the street, which are orientated towards the outside or inside of the block. As for the high-rise apartments, the street changes form depending on level: at ground level it is a roofed inner street in two and three layers that gives access to maisonettes. Between the second and the fifth storeys it is a corridor leading to apartments. The apartments on the sixth floor are accessed from an open inner street again: a rooftop street flanked by detached and semi-detached housing units in two storeys. A double system of stairs winds its way through the streets and links all the floors together.

6

1 ground floor
2 second floor
3 sixth floor
4 cross-section tower block
5–6 model

4

5

3

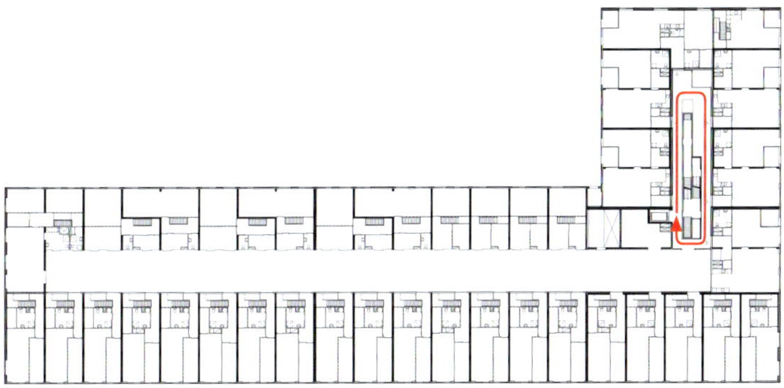

2

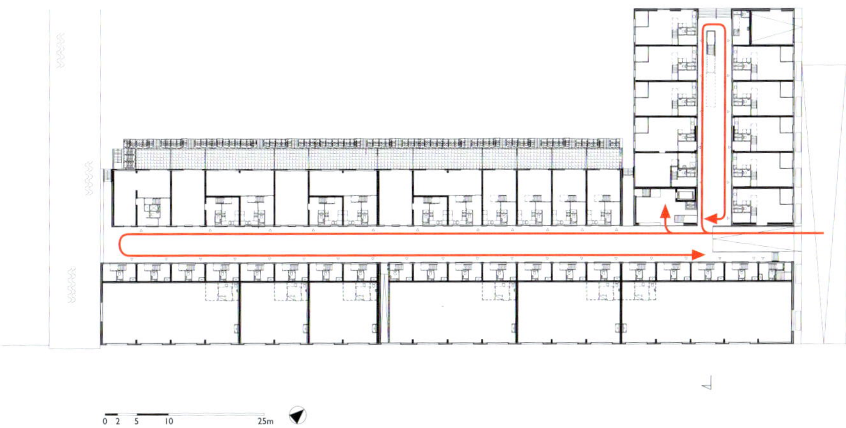

1

IV Residential care centre, Berkenstede, Diemen

The form of the Berkenstede care centre is largely defined by the compulsory urban planning condition that from the second storey the building must consist of four separate volumes. To avoid the cliché of a flat box with four towers on top, the upper and lower parts of the building have been inseparably linked together and the four volumes stand one behind another like stage sets, connected by an elongated inner street.
On the outside the blocks form a miniature town of high and low buildings. Between these buildings lies a hidden landscape with gardens, terraces, patios and slopes. The inner street provides a clear orientation within the complex, and from here the different sections of the care centre are visible and accessible. As a counterpart to the public inner street, there is a service corridor on the first floor that connects all the care and residential areas with one another. Both in the straight inner street and the meandering corridor above, shifting views of the patios and gardens provide spatial orientation. Since the lower floors of the building are transparent too, it lacks the usual hermetic character of a care centre.
The four towers with the residential and care areas differ from one another in building height and in the façade material. Roofs and the sloping façades are finished in different materials on each tower: zinc, slate, grass, wood, and creeper.

4

5

6

1 situation
2 diagram of organisation with four towers
3 diagram:
A zinc, B patio, C wood, D pond, E grass, F slate
4–6 scale model photographs
7 sketch of inner street

1

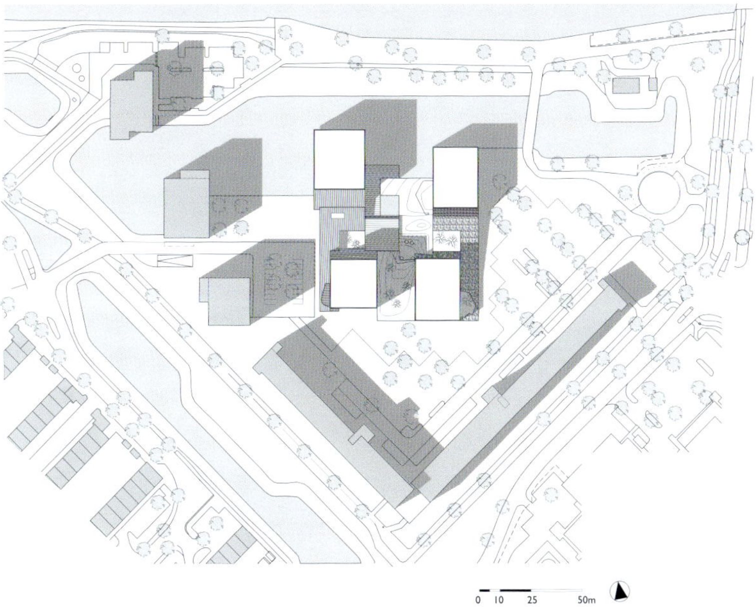

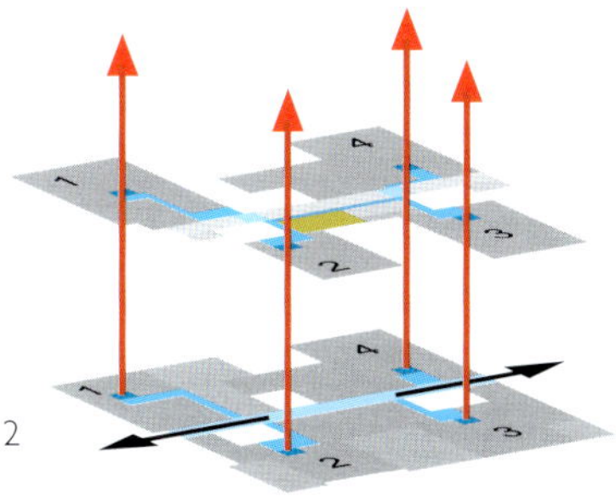

2

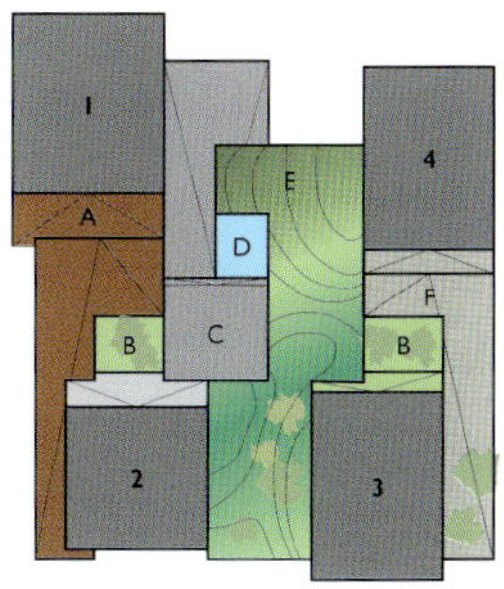

3

7

4

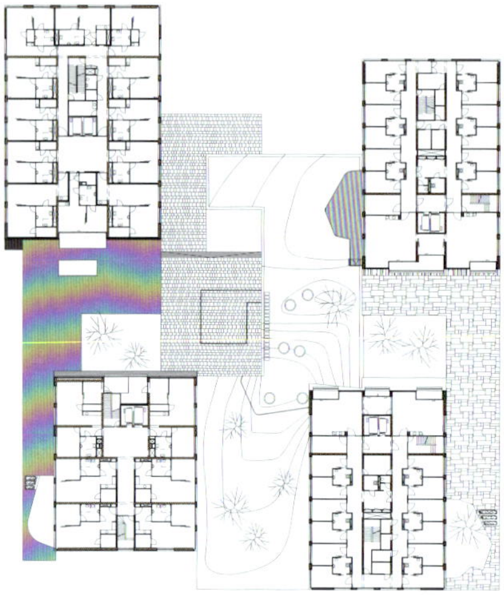

2

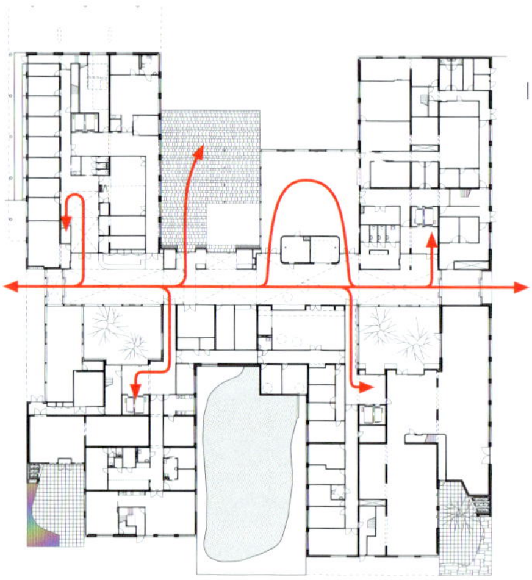

1

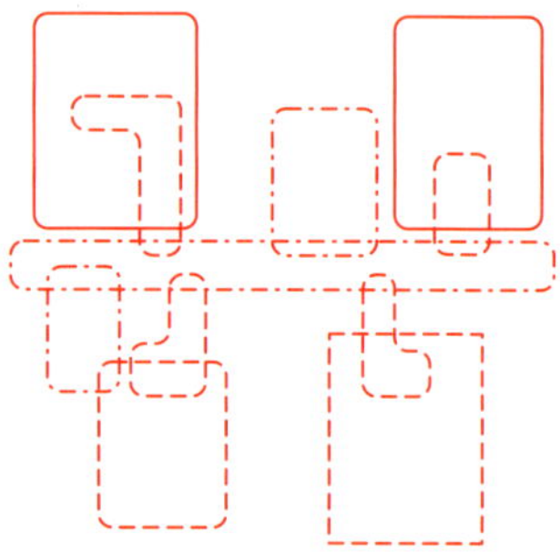

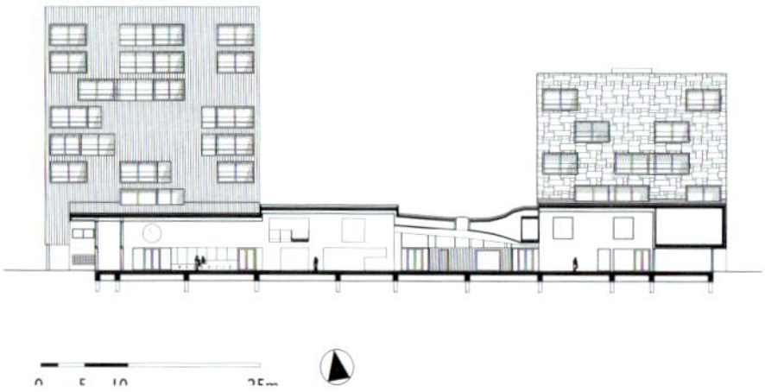

3

1 ground floor
2 second floor
3 cross-section of inner street
4 model

V Houtrust competition, The Hague

Houtrust, once a country estate on the outskirts of The Hague, is now a residual area between the Bosjes van Poot and two residential districts, Vogelwijk and Statenkwartier. The planning zone, together with the adjacent sports grounds, is conceived as an open plantation of fields and tree-lined avenues bordering the dune woods. Six blocks of apartments follow the geometrical arrangement of the area and maintain its open character by being positioned as close to the edge as possible. They are arranged in two groups on a continuous plinth that accommodates the car parks, entrances, storage areas, a school, a sports complex, and an existing squash hall. The tower blocks have been arranged in such a way that virtually every apartment has a view of the fields, the dunes and the canal. Moreover, the residents in the adjacent neighbourhoods can still enjoy a partial view between the tower blocks. The 'wild' dune vegetation makes its way into the site and continues from the square at the front of the complex via the forecourts and patios to the roofs. The geometrical structure of the fields for sports facilities and buildings can be seen from the rows of trees that line the avenues and paths between the fields and buildings. The 'pure' and modified forms of nature intertwine.

1

2

3

1 bird's-eye view
2 view from football fields
3 view from other side of canal

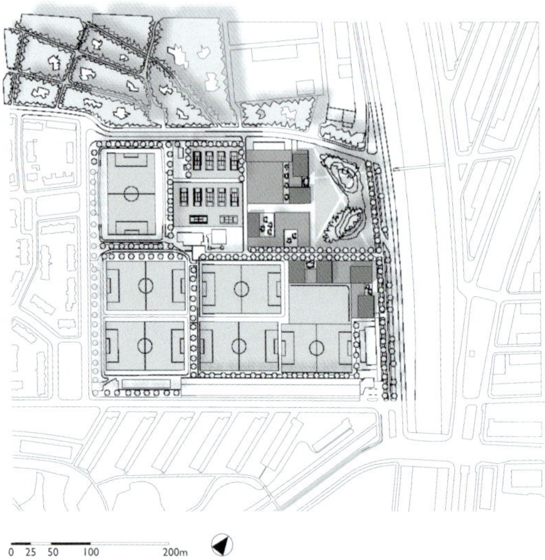
0 25 50 100 200m

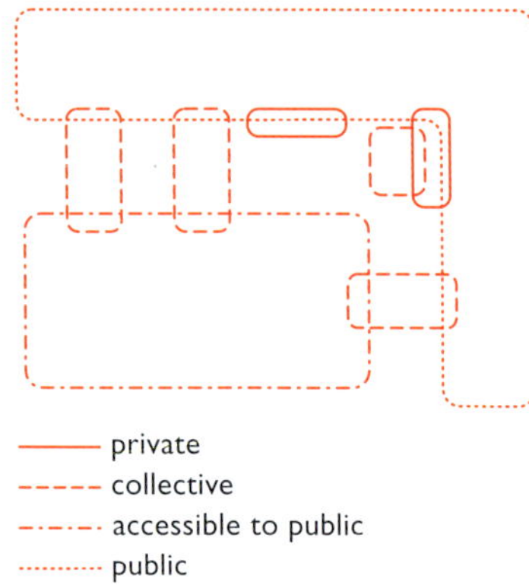
private
collective
accessible to public
public

5

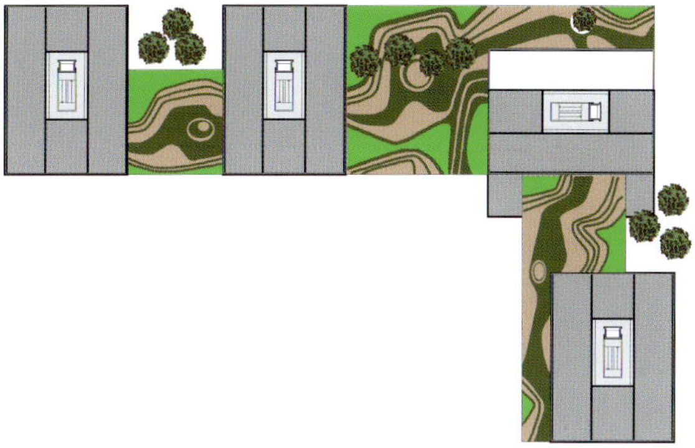

3

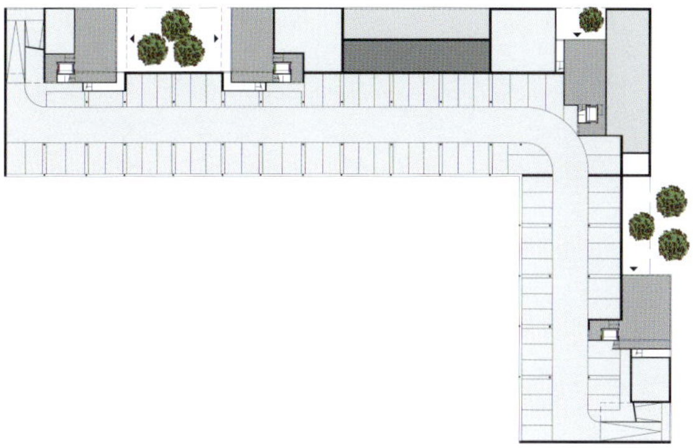

2

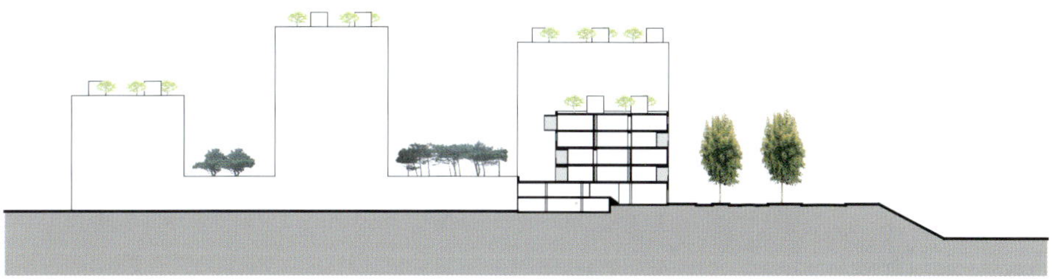

4

1 situation
2 ground floor of southern apartment block
3 apartment level
4 cross-section
5 seen from north
6 view from balcony

6

VI Zuiveringspark, Amsterdam

The concrete storage tanks in Oostoever, a residential neighbourhood on the site of the former sewage treatment plant, have been integrated in a housing project on the park-like strip in the middle of the new estate. Buildings have been concentrated as much as possible close to the concrete remains of the purifying plant. The rest of the space is used for a green field that joins the Sloterpark and thereby connects the new neighbourhood with its surroundings. Public, collective and private green areas alternate in the strip, separated by the concrete remains of the purifying installation. The project consists of 89 homes. Apart from the seven apartments that have been accommodated in one of the three drums, these are situated in two volumes: a seven-storey strip that emphasises the length of the green strip, and an eighteen-storey block at the end of the strip. Both blocks stand against and on the concrete purifying tanks, which function as collective gardens for the residents of the apartments as well as providing parking and storage space. Large holes that have been sawn out of the concrete walls of the existing buildings establish a relation between the public and the collective space. A number of these openings are closed by fences designed by the artist Peter Schoutsen.

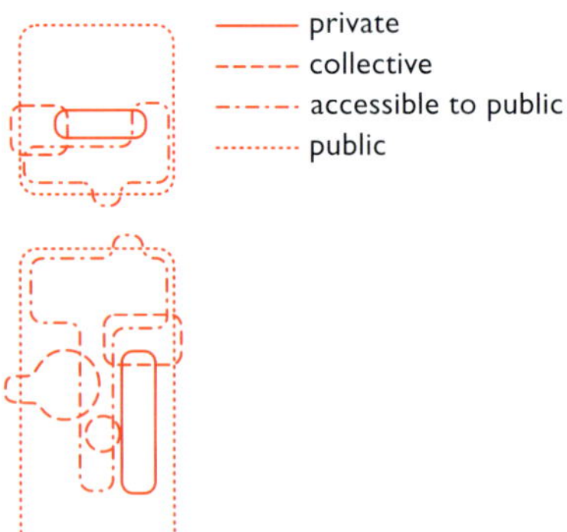

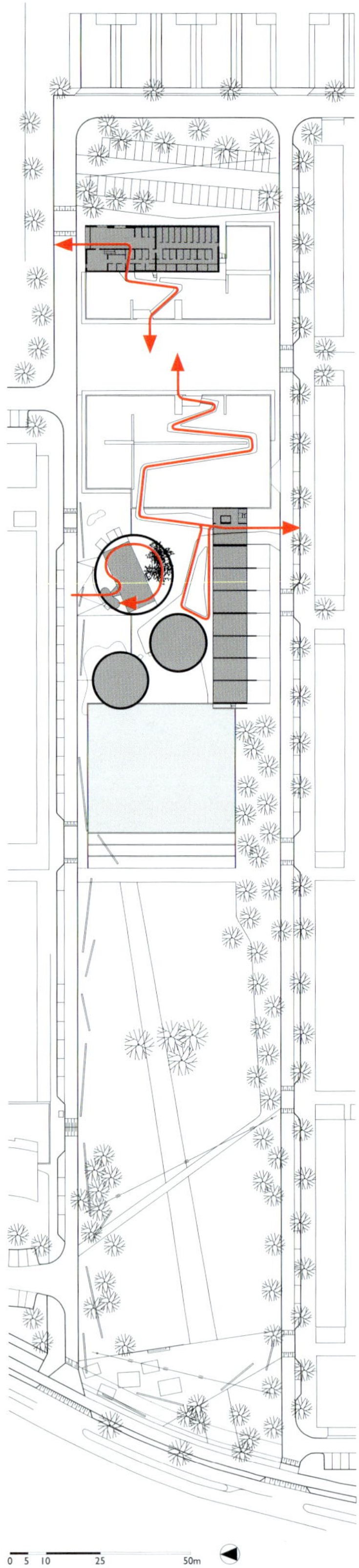

3

2

1 situation

2 original situation

3 view from drum towards apartment tower block

1

2

3

4

5

1 apartment block on purifying tanks
2 view between drum and low-rise apartment block
3 drum with apartments
4 seen from tall apartment block
5 pond between park and buildings

VII Urban study, Moerwijk, The Hague

The postwar part of the Moerwijk district in The Hague consists almost entirely of standard blocks of flats, in strips of two to four storeys. Only the clusters with services interrupt the uniform structure of the district. A plan has been developed for one of these clusters. This location, which is divided into five plots, consists of three schools, a church and church buildings, and a former convent. In the middle is a hidden square that forms the entrance to the church. The square is bordered by walled schoolyards and by the garden of the former convent. The plan retains the specific spatial character with concealed squares, courtyards and walled green areas to reinforce the contrast with the surrounding open building structure. On each plot the buildings have been replaced by a four-storey block and a walled garden or stone courtyard. The position of each block takes the greenery that is already in position into consideration, and most of it has been left intact. The church is turned into a walled garden. The outside walls of the church are retained as façades for three new blocks. The apartments in the blocks are grouped around light shafts and passages that connect the walled gardens and squares with one another.

6

5

1 situation
2 church building in 1955
3–4 model
5 northwest corner
6 square

2

0 5 10 25 50m

1

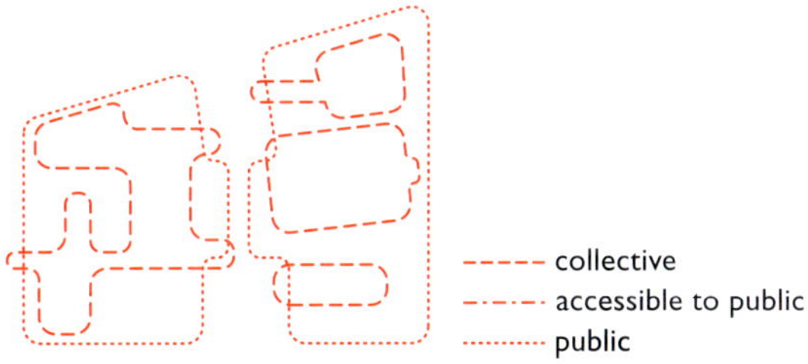
collective
accessible to public
public

3

NIENOORDSTRAAT

4

VIII Housing, Huizen

These three housing blocks are the latest addition to the residential district beside the Gooimeer on the northern side of Huizen. Three blocks, each with sixteen apartments and six ground-level houses, are placed among a variety of small-scale houses. Garden walls link the three volumes and make them into a whole. Three gateways in the garden walls provide access to a path that is open by day and can be closed off at night. This path forms a link right through the block. It is flanked by the blocks, the private gardens of the ground-level homes, and the collectives gardens of the apartments. A parking facility is incorporated in each of the three blocks at ground level. Despite the limited building height of three storeys, a density of seventy housing units per hectare has been achieved, which is twice as much as what is conventional in expansion districts.

6

5

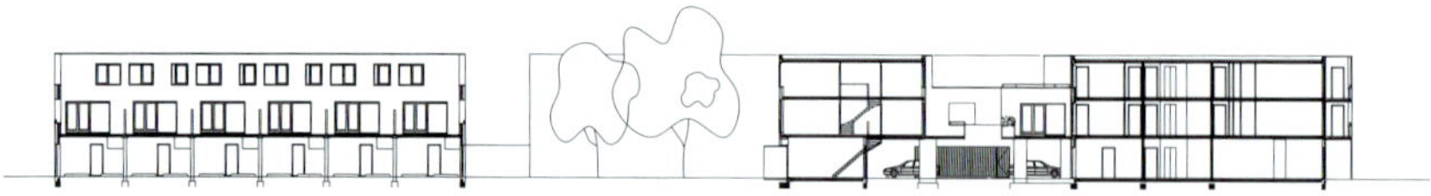

4

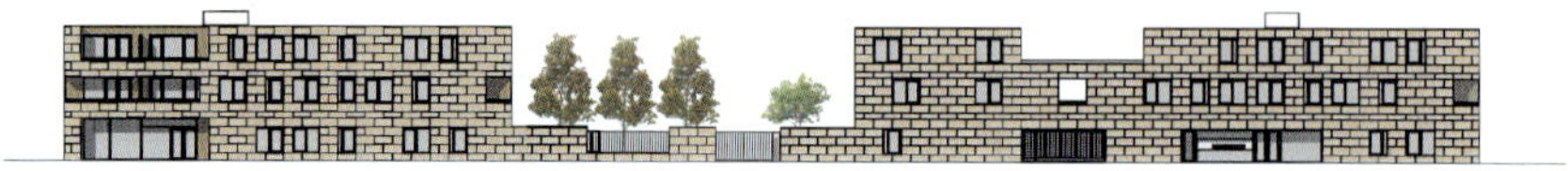

7

3

2

1

1 situation and ground floor housing blocks
2 first floor housing block
3 second floor housing block
4 cross-section
5–6 model
7 southwest façade

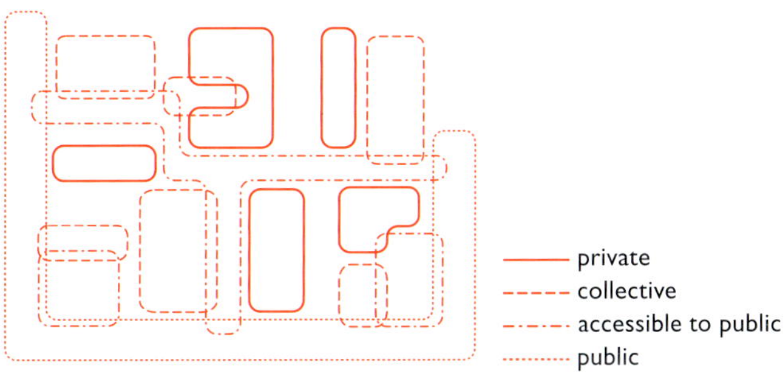

III The Interweaving of Building and Space

Spatial and functional diversity, density and privacy are not only closely interconnected in buildings in an urban setting, even though that is often where the interconnection is at its most manifest. On a different scale, the same theme also plays a crucial role in the design of suburban residential estates. The densities there are lower than in the city, but when it comes to grouping homes and apartment blocks in a suburban setting, the connection and separation of private, collective and public areas is just as important as in the case of an inner city complex.

One of the earliest green suburbs, **Hampstead Heath Garden Suburb**, situated on what was the margin of London a century ago, has had a major influence on the development of suburban housing. With a density of no more than twenty homes per hectare and a uniformly middle-class population, it is unsuitable as a model for present-day requirements. Nevertheless, Hampstead Heath Garden Suburb is still an interesting catalogue of spatial models for the arrangement of homes in relation to one another and to the open space around them. The most important condition for a suburban housing estate is probably that the landscape is visibly present. Otherwise, the suburb is nothing, lacking both the functional and spatial dynamism of the city and the relaxed character of open green spaces.

A stone's throw from one another, houses in Hampstead Heath Garden Suburb are linked with the open space in two radically different ways. In the oldest part of the estate, the houses are separated from the landscape by a wall. This Great Wall separates the back gardens of the houses from Hampstead Heath. Garden pavilions and sheds have been incorporated in this wall like medieval watchtowers. The only openings in the wall are where one of the main streets of the Suburb leads to the Heath to provide pedestrian access to it.

Southwest of the Great Wall, along Hampstead Way, is the first expansion of the Suburb. The opposite approach was adopted here. The houses are grouped around closes that open directly onto the open expanse of the Heath. These closes have been implemented in a number of variants. The proposals by M.H. Baillie Scott are interesting, in which the closes are articulated as autonomous collective spaces by means of differences in height and low walls. The architecture of the surrounding homes is designed as a total composition to which the individual home is subordinated. This idea was taken furthest in Waterlow Court, a complex with small single apartments for unmarried women, where the close is a closed courtyard. A long roofed passage establishes the connection between the courtyard and the open space.

Interest in a meticulous elaboration of the relation between the home and its surroundings can also be found in many Danish housing plans. By comparison with the textbook examples of the English garden city movement, Danish housing estates are often organised more simply, but are extremely effective in evoking the suggestion of a continuous landscape. A typical feature of these plans is the use of long rows of terraced houses, a type of home that has been in existence in Denmark for centuries. The **Bakkehusene** project (1921–1923), west of the centre of Copenhagen, combines this Danish tradition of long rows with the principles of the English garden city. The strips of simple but carefully designed brickwork houses end in a central green area, a field bordered by double rows of lime trees. The strict organisation recalls the later *Siedlungen* in Frankfurt. Thanks to the large private front gardens and the walls that hide the back gardens from sight, however, the spatial and architectural effect of this design is less vulnerable than in the Frankfurt example.

Arne Jacobsen developed this idea in his beautiful housing districts of the 1940s and 1950s. **Islevvaenge** (1951) follows Bakkehusene in its pattern, but displays an even closer affinity with the *Siedlungen* in Frankfurt, particularly Westhausen, because the homes no longer face one another across the streets, but have an identical orientation.

Still, the layout of Islevvaenge is far more romantic. The straight lines of Bakkehusene and Westhausen have been bent to suit the gently rolling landscape. In the meantime the green garden partitions have hidden the low brickwork homes from sight and the architecture has been swallowed up by the green landscape.

A dilemma of the suburb is how the relation with the landscape can be maintained in the future, too. In most cases the adjacent landscape is a prime candidate for the next expansion. The question of how to retain the landscape in the face of further growth was an important research item for Team 10 architects like Jaap Bakema and the Smithsons.

At the tenth CIAM conference in 1956, Alison and Peter Smithson presented various housing models based on the Geddes Valley Section, developed by the visionary urban designer Patrick Geddes to show the coherence between settlement patterns and the landscape.

One of the Smithson's models, **Close Housing** – a clear reference to Hampstead Heath Garden Suburb – offers a solution for suburban housing. In this model one-family homes are brought together so that they combine to form a roofed passage which connects the homes as a public footpath. Small closes lead from this passage to the front doors of the homes. The sketch offering a view of the open landscape seen from the passage via the close is of crucial importance because it shows that density can lead to a closer relation with the landscape.

The homes are strung together to form long ribbons that follow the topography. The passages form a branched pedestrian network. The gardens of these houses

Hampstead Heath Garden Suburb, Hampstead Heath, London, UK

Raymond Unwin and Barry Parker

Early 20th century

5

1

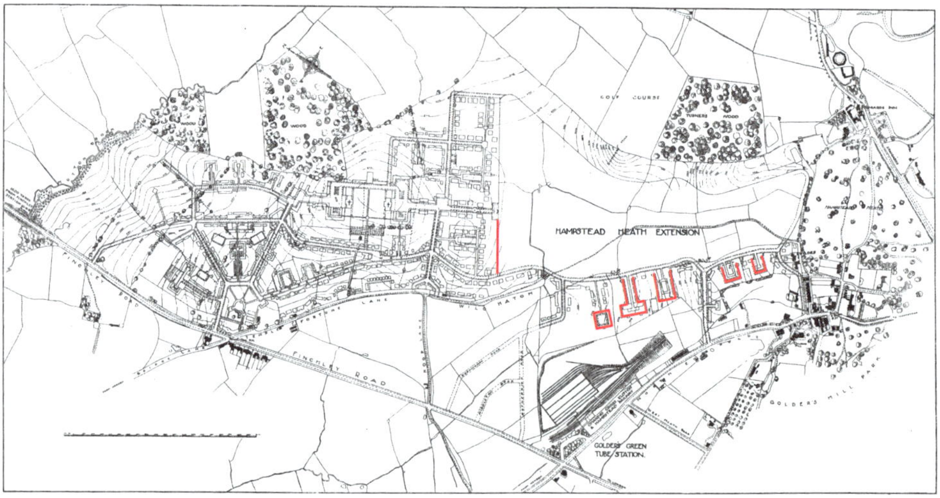

1 urban development plan of 1909
2 the Great Wall
3 Waterlow Court
4 close on Plot 400, not implemented
5 aerial view circa 1920

2

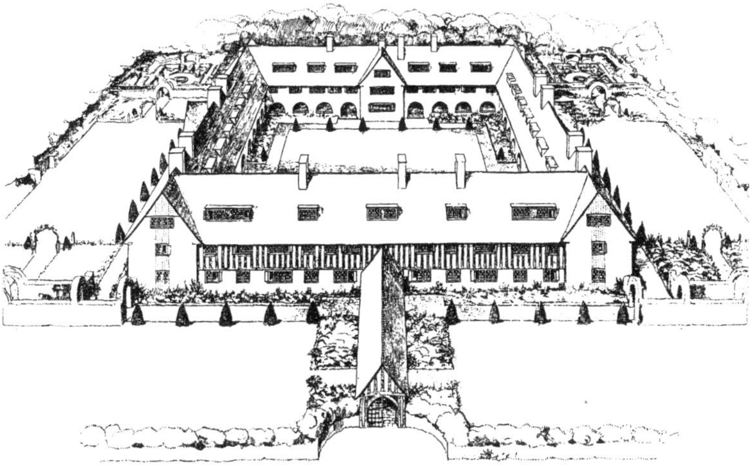

3

4

Bakkehusene, Copenhagen, Denmark
Ivar Bentsen; Thorkild Henningsen
1921–1923

1

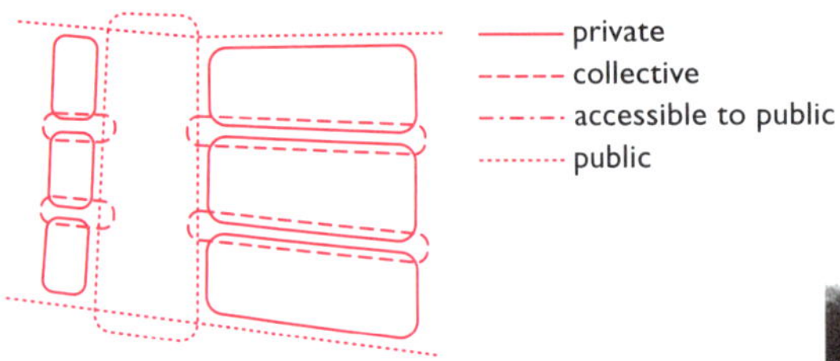

4

3

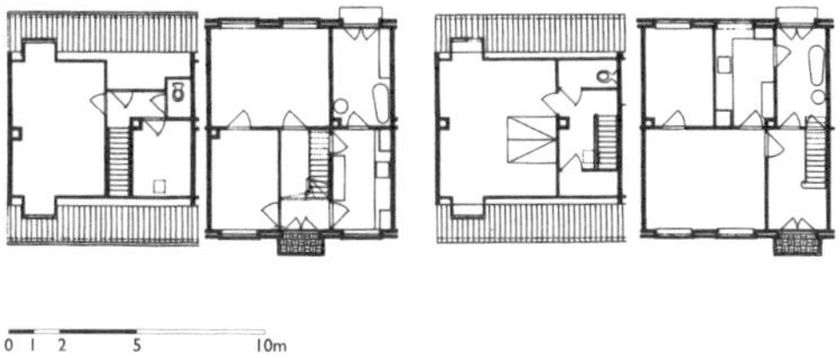

2

1 situation
2 typical plan
3 central field
4 street and houses

Islevvænge Rødovre, Copenhagen, Denmark

Arne Jacobsen

1951

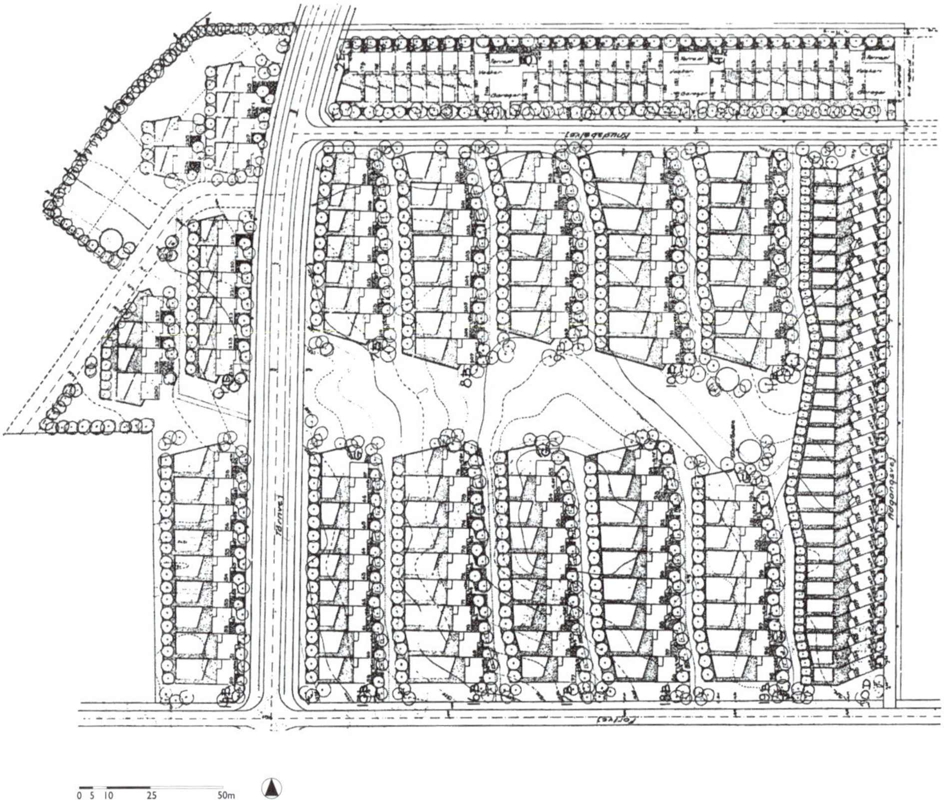

1

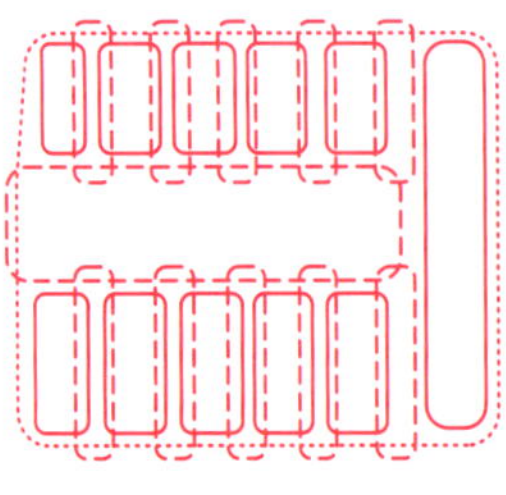

private
collective
accessible to public
public

5

3

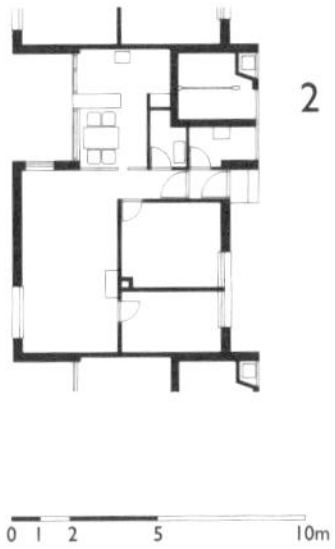
2

4

6

1 situation
2 typical plan
3 central field after construction
4 present situation
5 on the periphery
6 entrance side of the houses

The Valley Section Housing: The Close Houses

Alison and Peter Smithson

1954–1956

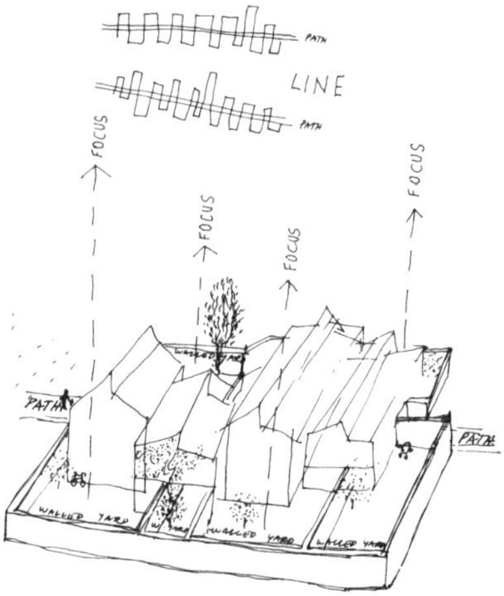

2

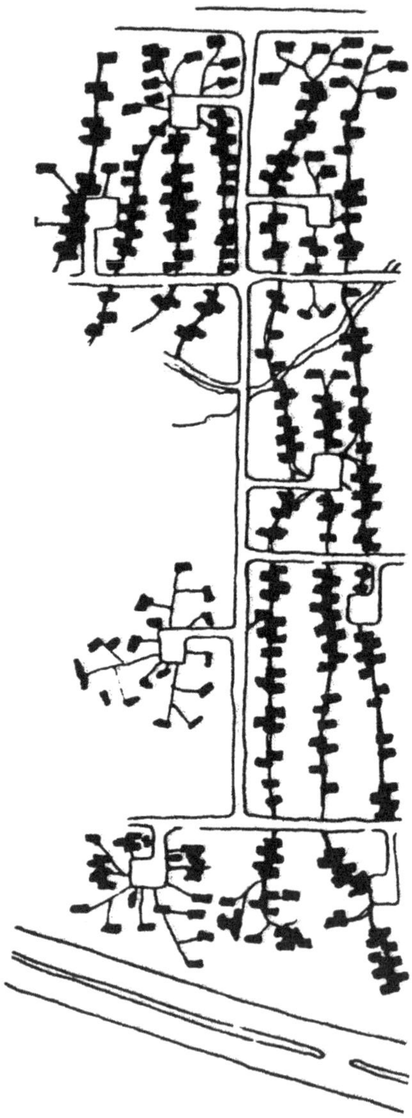

1

0 10 25 50 100m

4

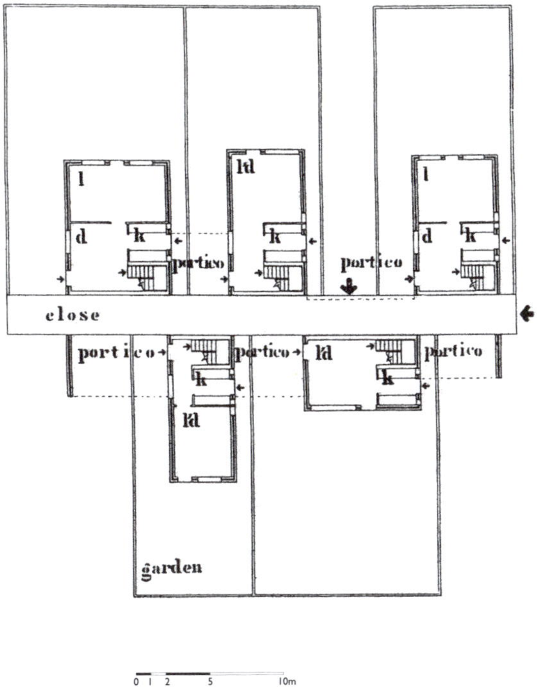

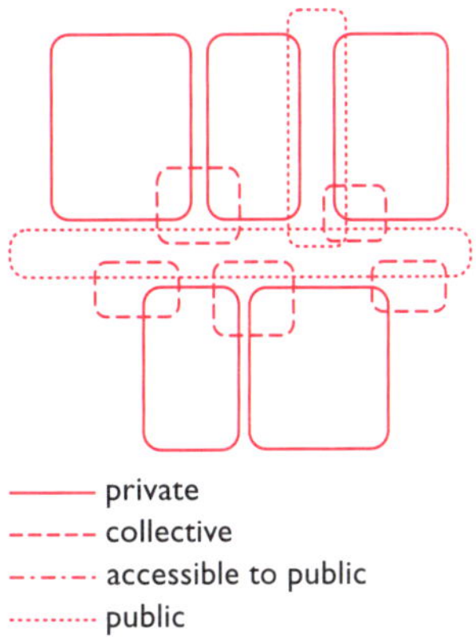

3

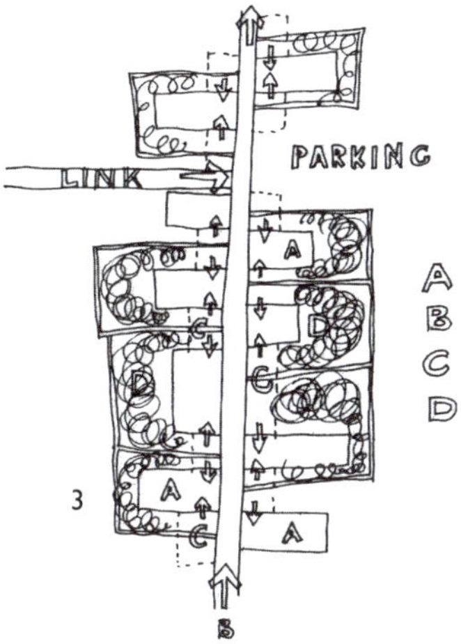

5

1 sketch of situation in landscape
2–3 sketches of cluster
4 ground floor of cluster of five houses around close
5 view from close via passage towards landscape

are separated by walls from the open spaces between the ribbons. However, it is noteworthy that accessibility for cars and parking facilities, which always played a key role in the designs of the Smithsons, have not been resolved here. The car is simply placed in the open intermediate spaces, thereby compromising the idea of the landscape that extends – at least visually – right up to the houses.

The car is a major problem when it comes to connecting home and landscape without any intervening obstacle. Another negative aspect, especially at the point in time when the number of homes per hectare increases, is that of the invasion of privacy. The dream of living by oneself in nature is disturbed if this nature has to be shared by many others in order to reach their own homes.

This gives rise to a remarkable paradox. To ensure adequate privacy for the suburban home, it is introverted, separated from the outside world by walls or closed outer façades, and thereby from the landscape.

At the beginning of the twentieth century, M.H. Baillie Scott was one of the first to attempt to develop a series of new housing typologies to reconcile the contradictory desire for privacy with a view. His book *Houses and Gardens* (1906) includes a plan for a row of **terraced houses** with gardens facing south. He presents this type with some scepticism, since, as he writes, it is doubtful whether a developer would find the proposal attractive, not because it is more expensive than the conventional types, but because it is unusual and goes against the accepted traditional plan of the terraced house, which leads to such irrational and what he regards as 'inartistic' solutions – words that have lost none of their currency today.

The ground plan of this house is an extremely compressed version of that of the large English country house, of which Baillie Scott's own design for Blackwell is an example (see p. 18). The service wing and the entrance are entered from a forecourt that is closed off from the street. The entrance leads to a large hall next to the garden, with open communication to a lower sitting area with a hearth and a dining table.

The forecourt is separated from the street by a wall that continues as the outer wall of the service wing. The result is a street wall consisting of nothing but a blind wall with a gateway every eight metres. In this way the house is completely isolated from the outside world. The interior and the walled back garden can maintain the idyll of the freestanding country home.

The plan performs the transformation from the detached house to the terraced patio house in one step. It thus resembles the Smithsons' close houses, which make the transition from a terraced house to a patio house with the introduction of closes and walled back gardens.

The patio house became very popular in residential suburbs in its terraced form in the 1950s. The hard and direct separation between the house and its surroundings, without front or back gardens to effect a transition to the public space, seems to leave the landscape intact. However, more than any other type of housing, the patio house shows the influence of increasing density. If density is low, the landscape can still penetrate the patio complex, as in many Scandinavian examples, most notably Jorn Utzon's Fredensborg (1959). When density rises, the landscape disappears from sight. Since the private greenery is also invisible behind the patio walls, what remains is a remarkable, petrified world.

If the landscape disappears, the quality of the architecture is the only decisive factor. This can be seen, for example, in the unusual **patio complex Ina Casa** with a high density that Adalberto Libera implemented between 1950 and 1954 in the Roman district of Tuscolano. From a distance this complex looks like a walled kashba or a Roman city liberated from the volcanic ash. At closer quarters the closed complex turns out not to be impenetrable and to contain a wide spatial diversity. The complex includes a cluster of shops where the closed outer wall suddenly gives way to shop windows. Between the shops is a large archway leading to a big open space in the middle, from which alleys lead to the patio houses. The entrances are grouped in fours around a widened part of the alley. In the centre of the complex is a small, four-storey apartment block. The building forms a strong spatial contrast with the surrounding low-rise buildings, but in functional terms it is a dubious element in the patio world and invades the privacy of the residents of the patio houses.

The most radical patio complexes have been designed by Serge Chermayeff. In the fascinating book *Community and Privacy* (1963) that he co-authored with Christopher Alexander, the patio house is presented as the ultimate answer to the demand for suburban housing. Diagrams in the book show how optimal privacy can be obtained in the patio house, not only with regard to the surroundings, but also between the members of a household. In addition, the authors claim that the patio house offers better protection against the acoustic and visual pollution of cars than any other type of home.

Chermayeff's patio plan for an **Urban group of houses** strings patios and private areas together. All of the areas are accessible via a corridor that extends throughout the entire depth of the extremely elongated building. Bedrooms and other rooms for parents and children are situated at opposite ends of the house. In between lies the shared living space where the members of the family interact. Each patio forms a buffer between the private and the collective area, and between the home and the street. The nine doors in the long corridor are also designed to reduce conflicts between the occupants and with the outside world to a minimum.

The design includes both a ground plan and a schematic division into plots. The houses fill a grid of footpaths in clusters of six. Cars have been relegated to a parking lot on the edge of the grid.

A Terraced House, project
Mackay Hugh Baillie Scott
Early 20th century

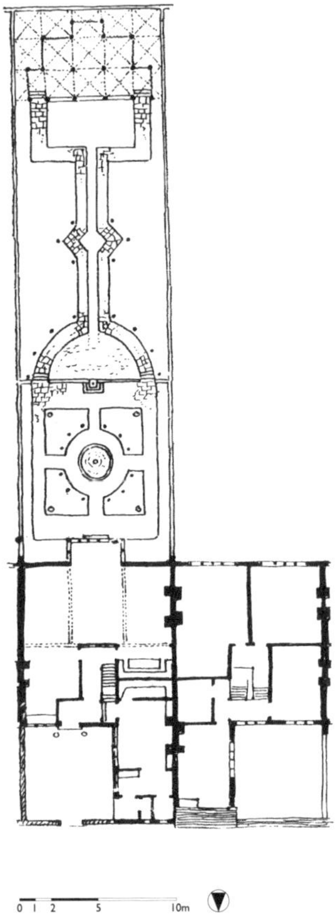

1

2

3

1 ground floor with garden and first floor
2 garden side
3 street elevation

Ina Casa Complex, Tuscolano, Rome, Italy

Adalberto Libera

1950–1954

1

4

3

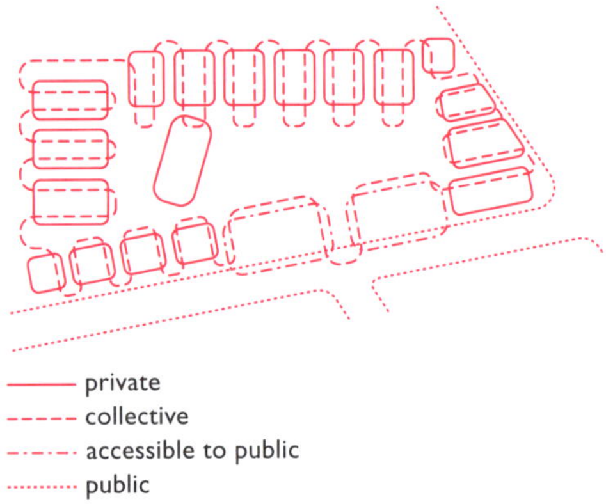

1 situation
2 cluster of four patio houses
3 shops on periphery of complex
4–6 alleys between the houses
7 aerial view

6

5

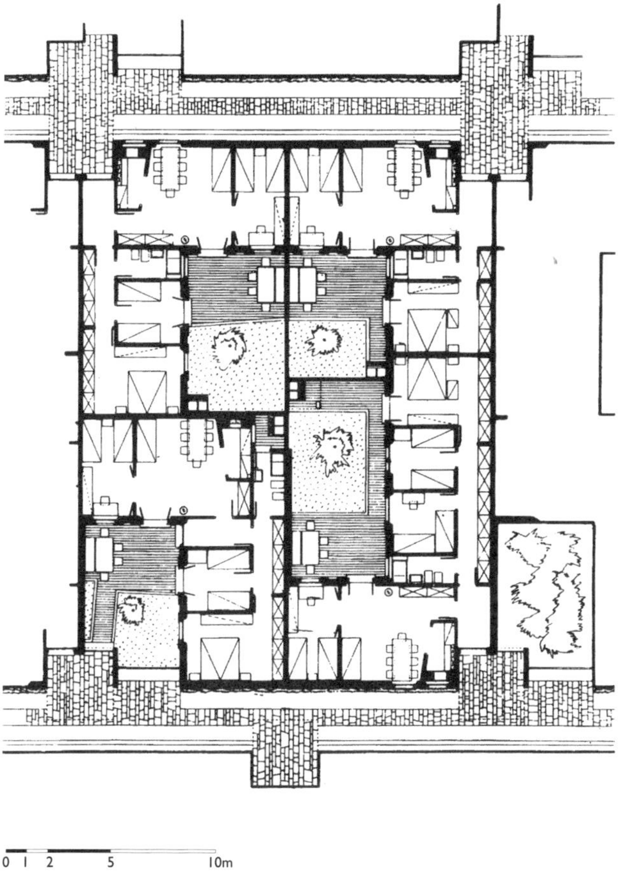

2

7

The literal implementation of Chermayeff's diagram would lead to a suburban nightmare that only makes one long for the classic US suburb with houses on green lawns beside wide tree-lined avenues. The house that he built for himself in New Haven in 1963 is a more practical embodiment of his vision. The patio design has here been elaborated to create a much more subtle version of the patio house, carefully embedded between the existing trees, in an otherwise traditional green suburb.

A design in which high density, adequate privacy, the relation with the landscape, and the inevitable presence of the car have been convincingly solved on a larger scale is provided by the **Span estates** in Blackheath, London. They are based not on theoretical schemes but on extremely pragmatic principles. The Span estates, built in the 1950s and 1960s, were developed by architect Eric Lyons and developer (and former architect) Geoffrey Townsend. Together with landscape designers Preben Jacobsen and Ivor Cunningham, they implemented a large number of housing projects both in and outside London in which they set out to *span* the gap between the monotonous English suburb and the country house setting that was beyond almost everybody's reach.

The main principles were density and adaptation. The plans aimed at the highest possible density to keep the price of the homes as low as possible. At the same time, the plans were fitted into the landscape with great care to retain as much vegetation as possible.

The Span projects usually consist of small rows of one-family homes in different sizes, or of small apartment blocks comprising two or three storeys. The flexible divisions into plots and the alternation of private and collective outdoor areas made it possible to preserve the landscape and its continuity even with densities of up to seventy homes per hectare. Cars were admitted in a casual way and were parked in small fields embedded in the landscape. The architecture is very simple; the façades are generally a collage of traditional building materials such as brick, wood and shingles.

The most striking Span projects are located in Blackheath Park. Until 1783 this area was an estate with a large stately home, but in that year it was sold to the developer John Cator, who demolished the stately home and divided the park into large plots of building land. After the construction of a number of avenues, increasing numbers of detached and semi-detached homes were built there from 1817 on. The character of the estate was preserved during this process of densification. The gateways at the edge of the park make it clear that the area forms a whole, while the wide green roads and large plots leave the idea of the landscape intact.

The addition of Span homes in clusters averaging forty units meant an enormous further densification of Cator Estate. The Span projects were often implemented in the back gardens of the nineteenth-century villas. Since the Estate was still entirely in the hands of the occupiers, the plan of the streets leading to the Span projects could ignore the local authority rules and regulations and be kept as simple as possible.

In this way the densification was able to proceed without affecting the character of Blackheath Park, so that its suburban character is not an illusion but a preserved reality. The success of Blackheath Park is largely due to the gradual development of the area, which has been an exemplary process of densification. That makes it different from practically every other suburb: they were developed in one go, have no scope for such transformations and densifications, and therefore often have only a limited shelf life.

Urban group of houses, project
Serge Chermayeff
1963

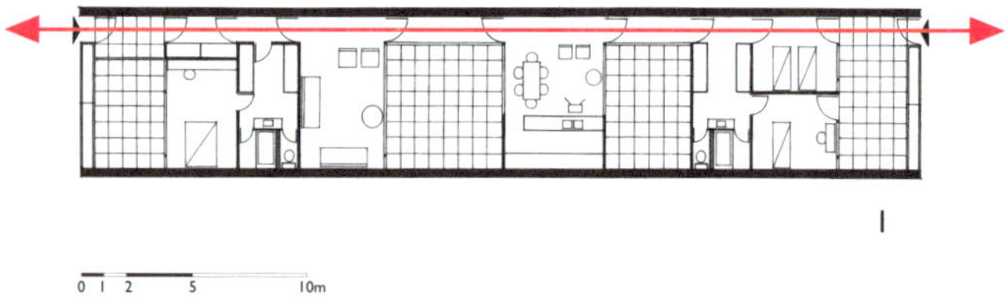

1

3

4

5

2

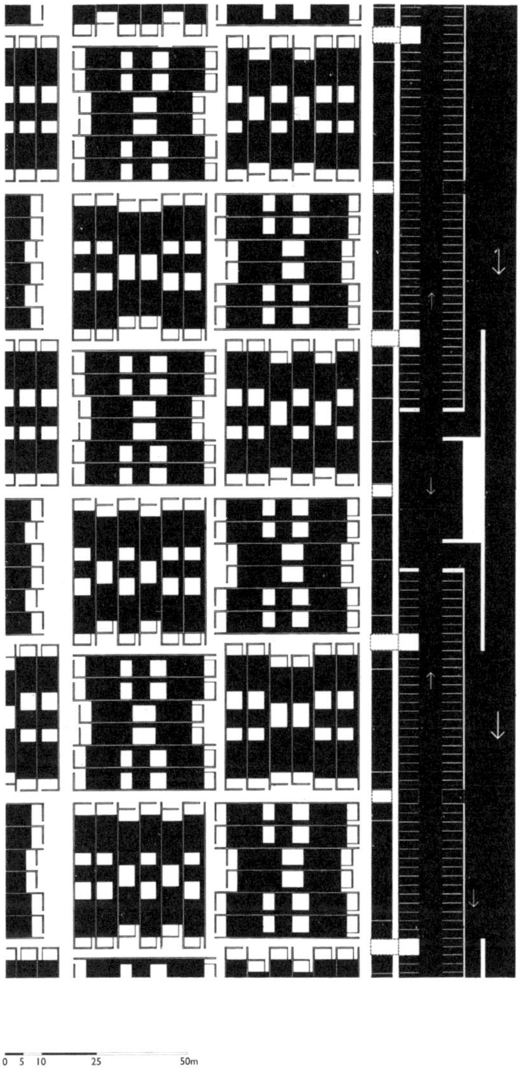

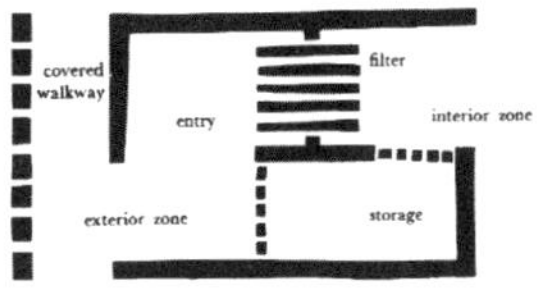

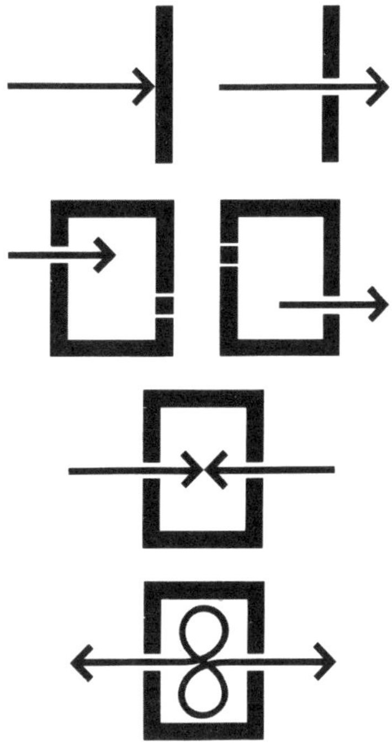

7

6

1 plan of patio house
2 layout of urban clustering
3–6 Chermayeff's own house, New Haven, 1963
7 diagrams from *Community and Privacy*

Span Housing, South Row, Blackheath, UK
Eric Lyons
1959–1963

6

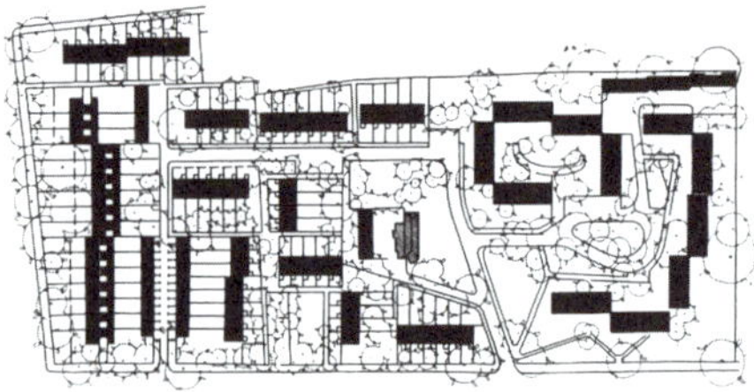

1

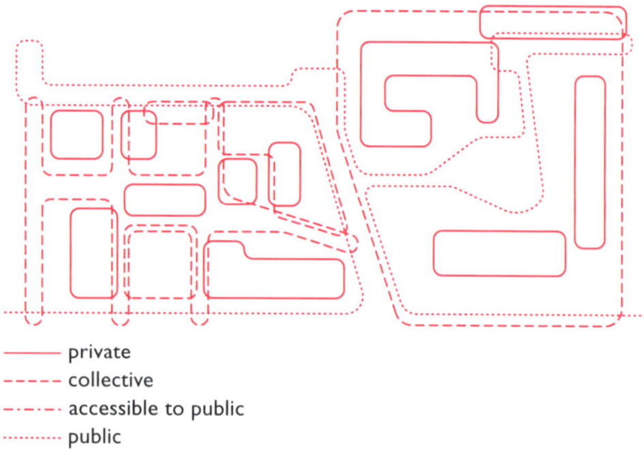

5

3

4

1 situation, the Hall
2 one-family houses, the Hall
3 one-family houses with patios, the Hall
4 plans of patio type
5 single-family houses, Corner Green
6 apartments, Hallgate

2

The theme of connection is at least as relevant to design assignments on the outskirts of the city as it is to the city itself. The residential suburb is by definition non-urban, and therefore requires the tactile or visual proximity of land which has not been built on. That it why it is necessary to interweave landscape and housing estate as far as possible. This calls for specific building layouts and housing typologies. Moreover, especially in the case of high densities, a finely meshed mixture of buildings, building plots and open land is required to maintain the suburban quality.

The interweaving of building and landscape rapidly falls prey to the desire to implement the maximal number of homes, each with a maximal plot of its own. This causes the disappearance of the potential quality of a residential suburb and results in a dull housing estate without urban complexity or a spatiality influenced by the landscape. That this dullness can be compensated by the architectural expressiveness of the façades is a regrettable and persistent mistake. The opposite is true: with increasing density, the architecture should be as inconspicuous as possible. The quality of the residential suburb, especially with high densities, is determined above all by spatial, not architectural diversity.

The interweaving of housing and landscape has been the guiding principle of several suburban housing projects. To achieve this interaction, the green vegetation on the edge of new housing estates has been extended as far as possible between the homes to create a maximal interface between the private plots and the collective and public green spaces. Examples of this are Grootstal and Ypenburg, where a large variation in housing typologies has been developed within a simple, continuous architectural and constructional structure. The same principle has been applied in the urban design for the Hedeman site, the transformation of a former industrial estate on the outskirts of Almelo.

The surface area occupied by green spaces is always highly restricted in suburbs for economic reasons. To prevent the scanty collective or public green spaces from being turned into fragments that could hardly be perceived as such any longer, the houses in Oosterhout have been concentrated to allow for maximal open green space. Moreover, they have been made narrow so that every house has a view of the open space. In every case the architecture of the houses has been subordinated to the design of the open space.

R R R R R R R
R R R R R R R
R R R R R R R
R R R R R R R
R R R R R R R
R R R R R R R
R R R R R R R

I Grootstal housing project, Nijmegen

The design of the public space occupies pride of place in this plan for one hundred and fifty ground-level rented council houses. The rigid linearity of the original urban plan has been modified by a series of shifts and inversions to create a variety of different kinds of public spaces. At right angles to these green areas are streets and parking lots orientated on a north-south axis. The housing units themselves are directly adjacent to the green intermediate areas which lead to the large strip of parkland that runs through the entire neighbourhood as an ecological zone. At ground level the public space has been kept as open as possible and has been laid out with grass, trees and narrow footpaths. The housing blocks form a tranquil background for this green residential area. The private back gardens are fenced off by masonry garden walls. On the other side, a concrete pavement separates the home from the public space. The façades of the rows of houses are all made of the same materials. Nevertheless, by making use of inversions and shifts, as in the modification of the urban plan, each block has been given a different look. The diversity continues behind the façades. Within a pattern of houses 4.80 metres wide with single pitch roofs, different types of home have been developed, each with its own spatial characteristics.

2

4

I situation

2 aerial view

3 wall and ecological zone

4 wall

3

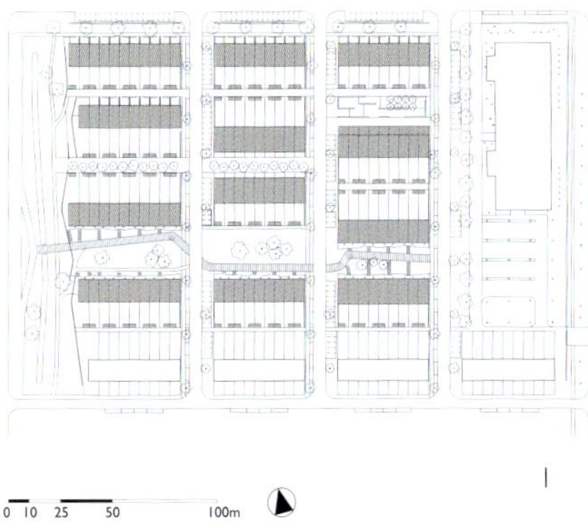
0 10 25 50 100m

1

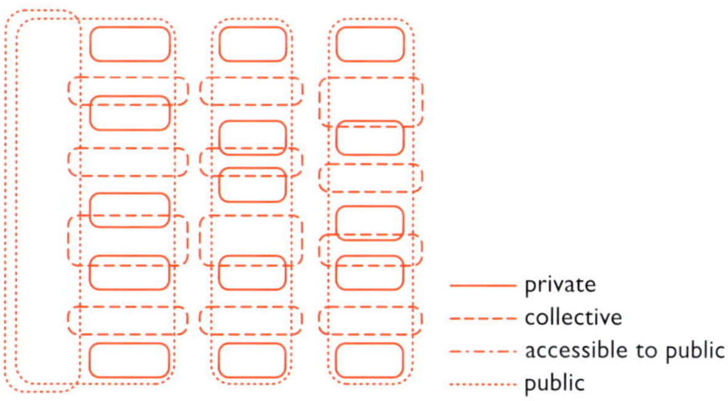
private
collective
accessible to public
public

1

5

1 green intermediate area
2 five housing types
3 interior type A
4 interior type D
5 interior type E

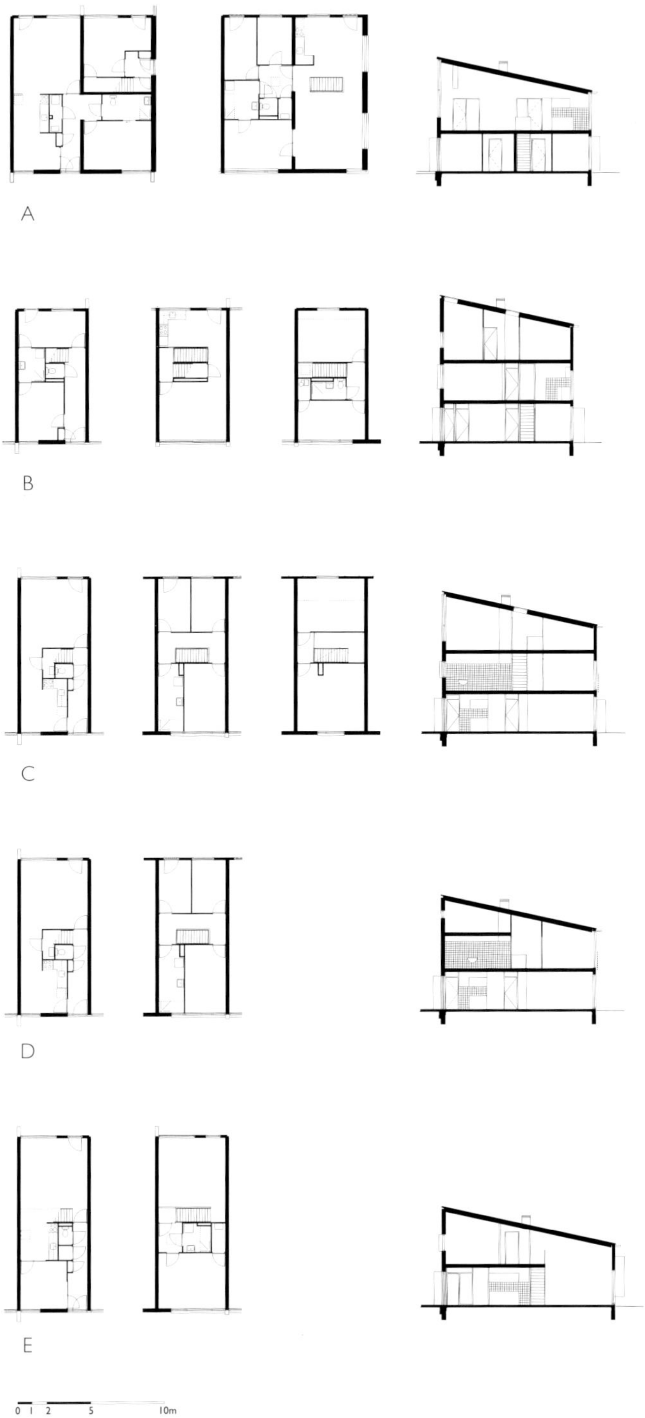

2

3

4

II Oosterhout housing project, Nijmegen

One hundred very inexpensive rented and owner-occupied housing units were to be implemented on a new housing estate full of traditional semi-detached houses north of Nijmegen. The location is divided by a wadi where rain water collects. By making narrow homes (no more than four metres wide), it was possible to give each of them a view of the central green strip with the wadi, and the number of roads could be reduced to a minimum. On the side facing the wadi, the homes have a terrace or open patio instead of a garden. The interiors of the narrow patio houses can be organised in a variety of ways, and there is potential for expansion on the roof. The homes are fairly inconspicuous because of the minimal size of the façades on the street side. This made it possible to argue convincingly that the architecture was able to ignore the prescribed aesthetics of pitched roofs and fascia board.

1

3

4

1 situation

2 cluster of patio houses with possible variations in ground plans

3–4 aerial view

5 green intermediate zone with wadi

5

2

III Hedeman site urban plan, Almelo

The Hedeman site is a former industrial estate, wedged between the old exit road with ribbon development to Ootmarsum and the Almelo-Nordhorn canal. The walled industrial site completely separated the adjacent neighbourhoods from the canal and from the rural landscape behind it. The design is based on a traditional division into parcels orientated in such a way that continuous lines of sight emerge between the canal, landscape and exit road. The homes on the parcels are situated alongside paths. Strips with gardens, paths and homes alternate with wooded embankments and wide ditches. Three loops make the strips accessible for cars. These loops lead into the surrounding old neighbourhoods, thereby linking the new buildings with the older districts. Besides, this also provides an immediate pretext to tackle the necessary renewal of these adjoining neighbourhoods. The central element in this plan, situated at the bend in the Ootmarsumsestraat, is a square with shops. Behind this paved square, which can also be used for markets, is a green square that is orientated towards the canal. A school is located beside this green area. Like the plan for Grootstal, which can be seen as a try-out for this way of filling the much larger Hedeman site, this design is determined by the linking of public spaces that are organised in different ways. Once again, the buildings occupy a subordinate position.

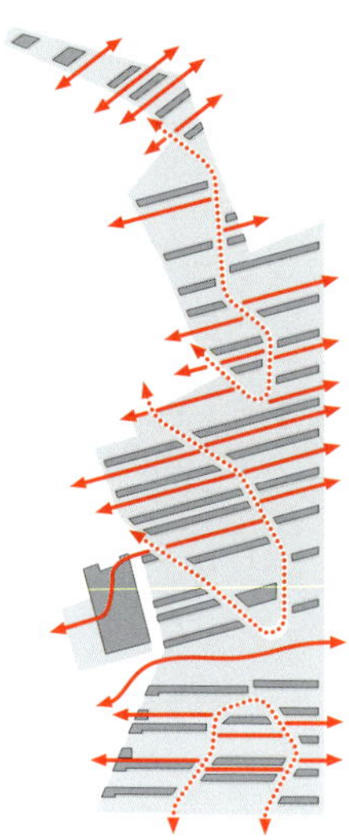

2

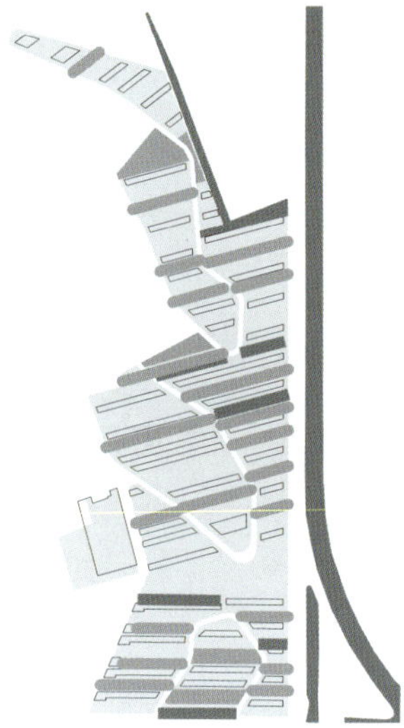

3

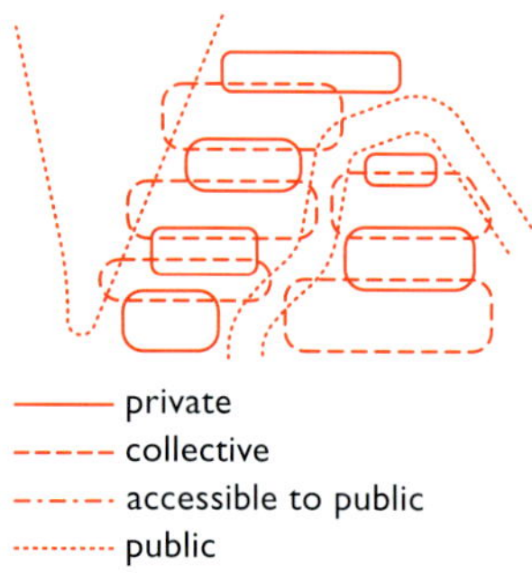

1 situation

2 diagram of streets and paths

3 diagram of vegetation and water

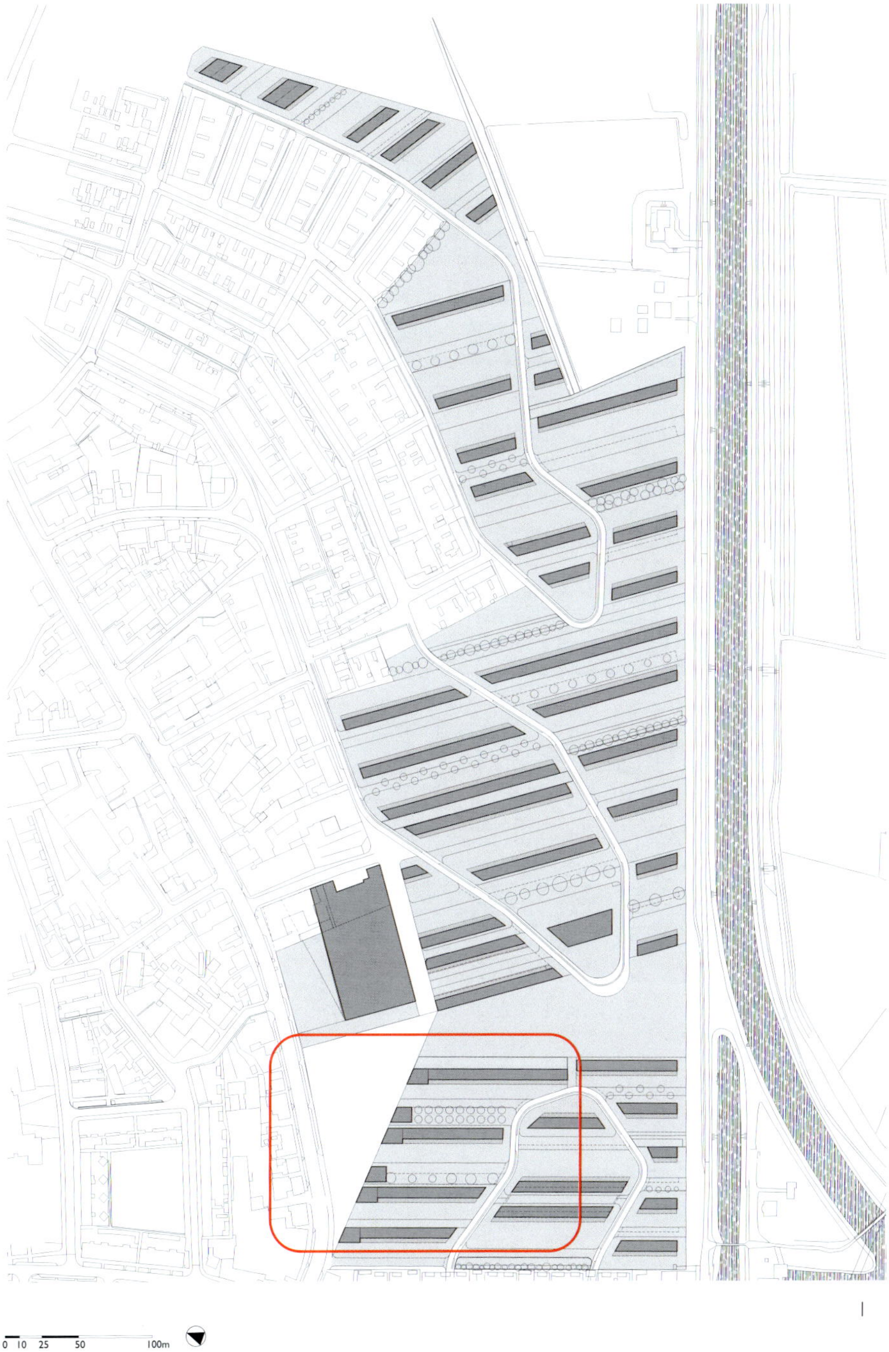
0 10 25 50 100m

4

5

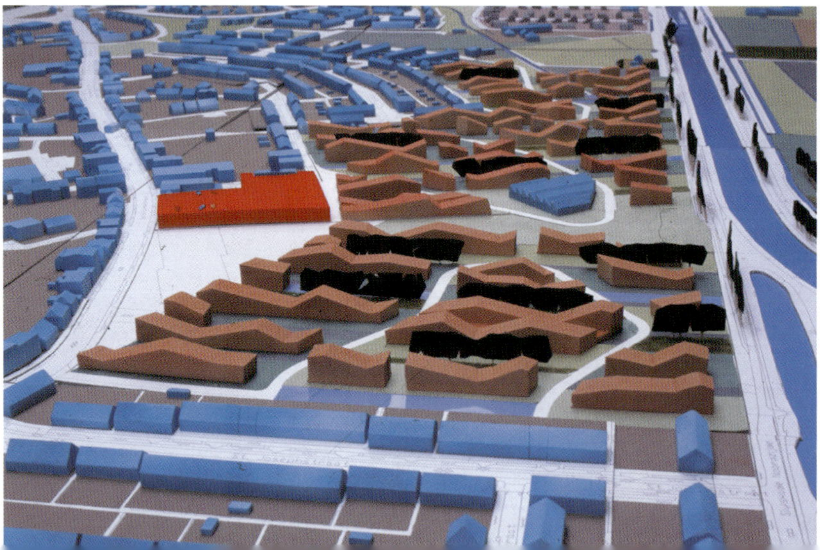

6

4–6 scale model

IV Singels II subsidiary plan, Ypenburg, The Hague

The basis of the plan for 650 homes at the end of De Singels, a part of the Ypenburg Vinex housing estate in The Hague, is the link between the district and its surroundings. The design was a commentary on the autonomy and introversion of most of the plans for parts of Vinex estates like this, which consist of archipelagos of subsidiary zones, each with a theme and characteristic of its own prescribed by urban planners and intended to create an artificial difference between virtually identical homes and neighbourhoods. The blocks of the Singels II subsidiary plan match the linearity of the adjoining neighbourhood, but fan out towards the green area at the end, thereby making it possible to orientate as many homes as possible towards the green margin and allowing the greenery to penetrate far into the neighbourhood. The roofs of the blocks have been designed to fit in with these contours. The roofs, with their tapering gutter and ridge lines reinforce the dynamism of the long terraces and confer unity on the different blocks. The façades conceal a diversity of housing types. The roof space is just as dominant in the interior as it is in the exterior. In most houses the attic space can be seen from the stairs. A limited number of materials, openings and colours have been used for the elaboration of the façades. This strengthens the continuity with the outdoor space. The design of the green intermediate spaces harmonises with the adjoining neighbourhood park. A system of footpaths along and between the blocks leads from the housing to this green perimeter. The streets are distinguished by their profile and by the different ways in which they have been planted with trees, not by the architecture of the houses.

1

2

1–2 aerial view

1

2

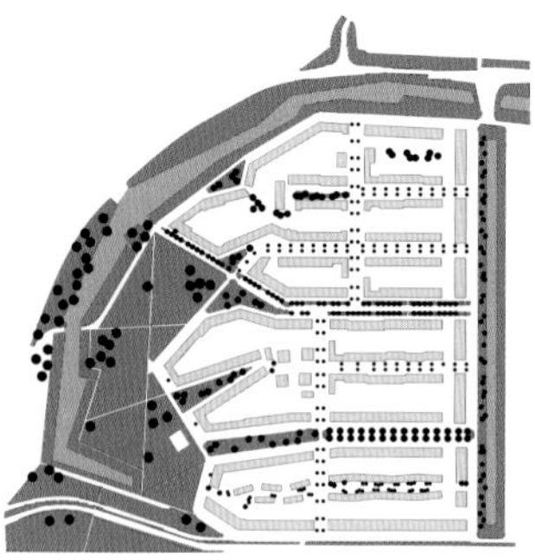

3

I situation

2 diagram of streets and paths

3 diagram of vegetation and water

4 six housing types

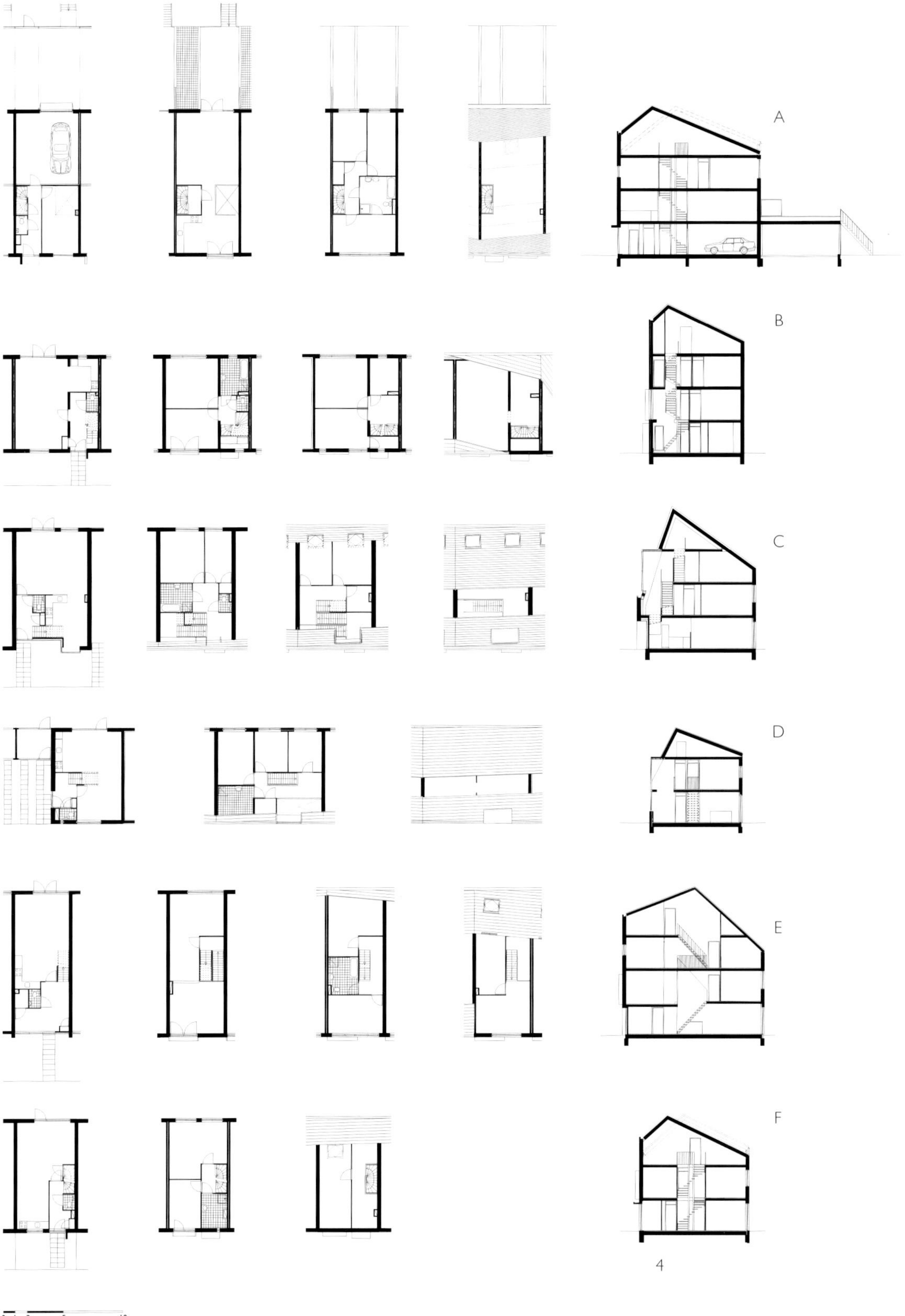

4

1

1 singel, type A

2 path beside green border, type C

3 street within block, type D

4 green zone with apartments at the corners

2

3

4

Afterword

This book is not based on some grand theory of architecture or some comprehensive vision of what architecture ought to be. It is first and foremost a practical reflection on the built environment, and specifically on its spatial aspects. The theme of the book is a way of looking at architecture and with it a way of designing. Its premise is spatial richness, not as an end in itself, but as a means of allowing a building or built environment to function in a more meaningful way: How can architectural space be offered (and left) for daily life?

This book is not about abstractions, but about tangible architecture and specific designs. It can be read in different ways: as a didactic manual for designers on how to deal with architecture; as an unconventional series of chapters in the history of the space in and around buildings; and as an explanation of an approach to architecture on the basis of the work of the author and of others.

Above all, however, it is a plea for an approach to the whole of architecture – the design assignment, the history of architecture, and dealing with existing buildings – that employs fine distinctions. A plea of this kind does not lend itself to bold statements, but that does not mean that this book is not based on a definite point of view.

Even if it is a 'gentle manifesto', to borrow the term that Robert Venturi used in 1966 to introduce his book *Complexity and Contradiction in Architecture*, the critique that lies implicit in *Revisions of Space* is a sharp one. That critique targets the one-dimensional approach to architecture as form, or more extremely, as concept, as well as the monofunctionality of many spaces in and around buildings, and with it the spatial impoverishment of much contemporary architecture. On the basis of historical and contemporary examples and his own work, Dick van Gameren shows how you can escape these pitfalls, and what spatial richness can mean for architecture and for those who use it.

If there is one aspect of architecture that is hard to describe, it is space. It is difficult to find the right words to refer with precision to spatial qualities. As a result, there is no part of architecture about which so many abstruse treatises have been written as space. The fact that it is so rare to find books written in a comprehensible and accessible way about what is undeniably an essential aspect of architecture is certainly also connected with the difficulty inherent in a precise perception of the space inside, between and around buildings. Gerrit Rietveld once said that when you look at architecture, the first thing you see is colour, followed by form, and only afterwards space. Whether there is a scientific explanation for this opinion or not, it is in accordance with how people generally talk and write about architecture – as well, apparently, as with how they look at it: space is often the last factor to be taken into consideration. Seeing the space and being able to grasp its significance require a way of looking that is free of the limitations of the first glance, in which architecture appears as material and form. At the least it calls for a second look, a look that goes further and that targets spatiality and movement through space.

This book is a successful attempt to describe what can be seen in architecture when one takes a second look. It is based on a large selection of examples from the distant and (very) recent past. These examples are not cited as arbitrary visual references – a practice that has become common in architectural circles – but they are treated analytically. Most of the historical examples are taken from North-West Europe, in particular the United Kingdom, reflecting Dick van Gameren's personal predilections.

The historical examples are not intended to provide supporting evidence for the quality of his own work as an architect, but can – and should – be taken as a putting in perspective and a sign of awareness that nothing is entirely new and without precedent. They can also be taken as an implicit general critique of the compulsive novelty that hangs like a halo round much (present-day) architecture. No matter how new or innovative many buildings may seem to be when viewed superficially, precedents can be found for many themes and motifs, whether the designers concerned realise that their work forms part of a specific continuity or not.

The critique of novelty is not so earth-shaking in itself. However, it does contain an element of going against the grain, especially today when so many architects are captivated by dashing forward and put their faith in the idea of the necessity of innovative inventiveness.

In terms of both form – the combination of historical examples with the author's own work – and content – the plea for variety and nuance – this book is undeniably related to Venturi's famous *Complexity and Contradiction in Architecture*. That work was published as the first – and after almost four decades still the only – volume in what should have been a series issued by the Museum of Modern Art in New York. Vincent Scully's preface already assumed that it would be an epoch-making work by presenting it without further ado as the most important book on architecture since Le Corbusier's *Vers une architecture*, which had been published more than forty years earlier.

The fact that this prophecy has come true is probably due less to the self-fulfilling effect of Scully's eulogy than to the unambiguous straightforwardness of the title of the book. Without having read a word of it, everyone can understand what *Complexity and Contradiction in Architecture* is about. And otherwise it is enough to read the first paragraph of the introduction to get the message. That is the great strength of the book, even though it is at odds with the main thrust of the argument.

The title of the present book does not produce such an immediate impact. In this respect *Revisions of Space* recalls one of Dick van Gameren's other favourites, the classic work by Serge Chermayeff and Christopher Alexander from 1963, *Community and Privacy*, whose title does not immediately make clear in which direction the book will take the reader either. At most, *Revisions of Space* offers some clues about what the reader can expect. It is about architectural space, and introduces alternative ways of looking. However, the title also alludes to the book and exhibition by Heinrich Klotz with which the Deutsches Architektur Museum in Frankfurt opened: *Die Revision der Moderne; Postmoderne Architektur 1960–1980*. That was the second review of postmodernism after *La presenza del passato*, the international architecture exhibition of the Venice Biennale in 1980. This postmodern architecture went out of fashion remarkably quickly, and it is not yet old enough to become timeless. Now that the element of surprise is gone, it becomes clear to what extent the postmodern symbolism was often lacking in subtlety, how superficial the anti-modernism was, and how arbitrarily historical references were used. That does not alter the fact that postmodernism has been responsible for a number of important contributions. The way in which postmodern architects, critics and historians have opened our eyes (again) to the rich diversity of history is of lasting value. As a result, since the late 1970s interest has arisen in what until then had been neglected, forgotten or unknown parts of the architectural past. This interest has led not to a systematic redefinition of that history, but to an adventurous roaming through the past, though often with an anti-modernist undertone, because the focus was primarily on architecture that fell outside the (modernist) historiography which was prevalent at the time. Nonetheless, that has hardly altered the weakness that seems to be inherent in architectural history and criticism: that it consists to a large extent of repetition and thus of confirming what has already been said or written. Consequently, reputations are based to a large extent on *positive feedback*, which makes what is important even more important, and what is unimportant even more unimportant.

Dick van Gameren manages to avoid this pitfall, at least partly, by also focusing on architecture that is regarded as unimportant from the perspective of the historical canon. It is undeniable that he has a wide knowledge of architectural history, more than that of many historians of architecture. His knowledge is not limited to the classics, but extends to the architects who are situated on the periphery of the history books because their work has not changed the course of history, or because they did not create an architecture that was unprecedented for its time or could be considered representative of a trend. That does not mean, however, that the buildings and designs are insignificant, but only at most that they hold up the main story too much.

Revisions of Space is a plea to look in a different way not just at architecture but also at conventional writing about the history of architecture. In spite of the liberty Van Gameren takes in dealing with history, he does not entirely shake off the hierarchy that is enshrined in the conventional histories of architecture. Not only is his knowledge of history determined by those conventional histories, but the selection of historical examples for this book also reveals an almost demonstrative recalcitrance, though this in no way reduces his genuine fascination by the buildings and designs he has chosen.

Pride of place is reserved in this book for various architects who are only known to insiders. It does not touch on twentieth-century big names like Mies van der Rohe, Le Corbusier or Alvar Aalto, and when well-known architects are discussed, it is their less well-known work that comes in for consideration.

Moreover, Van Gameren's view of the (more) well-known buildings is not a conventional one. His interest in the early work of Norman Foster focuses not on his technological inventiveness, but on the social space in one of his buildings. Likewise, his interest in Edwin Lutyens, a hero of the postmodernists, is motivated not by Lutyens' formalistic mannerism (which went down so well in the postmodern era), but by his skill in deploying space. The same goes for the work of postmodern masters like Venturi and James Stirling; Dick van Gameren chooses to discuss the latter's Neue Staatsgalerie in Stuttgart, a must in the mid-1980s, but today an almost forgotten architectural landmark. The circle is complete with Van Gameren's postmodern view of postmodernism itself.

The vision on which this book is based is postmodern without bearing a trace of anti-modernism. Nor is the architecture to which it gives rise stylistically related at all to postmodernism. Dick van Gameren's work does not contain any showy imitations, citations or pastiches. That work, and the argument of this book, reflect above all the awareness that the history of architecture is not just something that belongs to the past, but that it can be a valuable source of inspiration for new architecture. Equally postmodern is Van Gameren's preference for architecture that contains a multiple of meanings, layers and nuances. In the context of today's competition between conceptual one-liners and the need for every sensation to outdo the previous one, such an unfashionable viewpoint is a sign of a strongly autonomous position.

In 1984 Dick van Gameren was an architecture student at Delft University of Technology, where modernism was still the rage, and where almost no one was ready for a revision of modernism. The most important – public – moment of revisiting modernism in Delft did not come until the end of the decade, with the symposium 'How modern is Dutch architecture?' on the occasion of the departure of Rem Koolhaas as professor in Delft. Van Gameren had already graduated by then.

There is no denying that he was trained in the Delft modernist tradition. At the same time he has also been shaped by postmodernism, even though there was hardly any attention devoted to it in the Delft curriculum. On the one hand, his interest in architectural space can be called pre-eminently modernist. Space does not seem to have played a role of much importance in postmodern architecture, where the focus was almost entirely on the symbolic form (or at least a form that could be interpreted symbolically), under the banner of architecture as a bearer of signification. On the other hand, his handling of the history of architecture as a source of knowledge and inspiration for spatial solutions would be hardly conceivable without the liberating effect of postmodernism. The plural in the title of the book can also be taken as typically postmodern: a calling into question of the arrogant pretension of an overarching revision.

Dick van Gameren's interest in the spatial dimension of historical architecture was already evident during his time as a student from his involvement in Max Risselada's research project '*Raumplan* versus *Plan Libre*'. While that project was concerned with the analysis of the concept of space of two big names who have a permanent place in every modern history book, *Revisions of Space* shows that he has developed a taste of his own in the meantime, in which he reviews the work of established architects and often abandons the well-trodden paths of the historical canon to investigate work that often receives very little attention at all.

Buildings and projects are not arranged in strict chronological order in this book, but their position in each chapter is designed to enable the argument about space to develop in a logical manner. This is a small indication of a great difference from the way in which architects and historians deal with history.

For historians, history is simply an end. The main activities for this purpose are the interpretation of historical reality, the writing and rewriting of history, the establishing of connections, and the tracing of developments. Even without a grand narrative or a sacred belief in progress, for most historians their discipline still consists of narratives that establish connections between the succession of people, objects and events. No matter how fragmented and lacking in direction they may sometimes be, texts by historians almost always display a development, if only in the form of the passage of time. That is why chronology always plays a major role in the history of architecture. In the last resort, most historical narratives can be reduced to a model of precursors, protagonists and followers, and – in reaction to them – antagonists. More importance is usually attributed to precursors and protagonists than to followers and antagonists. This book is different: not one of the historical examples is the first of its kind.

For architects, on the other hand, the aim is not to describe the past as accurately as possible and to do full justice to historical reality. For them, history is an instrument to be used subjectively for a design: a collection of examples that may come in useful when it comes to solving present-day design problems. Chronology certainly does not have to play a role of any importance when it comes to general themes such as movement through space, to paraphrase Nikolaus Pevsner's definition of a building. For however much architecture develops in technological, constructional and programmatical terms, this does not necessarily change the foundations of the discipline, such as the design of space and the creation of spatial connections and divisions. When it comes to these themes, an architect need have no qualms about viewing history as a reservoir of sources of inspiration of equal value, irrespective of the time and place in which they were implemented.

Many architects, however, pay little or no heed to the past. Of course, the history of architecture can be a dead weight. In the light of talented predecessors whom it is difficult if not impossible to emulate, almost every attempt to create a new architecture, an architecture that makes an essential contribution to what already exists, is virtually doomed from the start. The most simple way to keep out of the shadow of the great predecessors is to ignore them. This approach is in line with the modernist tradition of the *tabula rasa*: the designer shakes off the past in order to invent architecture all over again, a practice that has gained in popularity in the recent supermodern years.

There are also architects who want to legitimise their own actions by appealing to the past, using the proven qualities of historical architecture and tradition as unassailable arguments for continuing to build on what has gone before. This traditionalist position was once characterised by Léon Krier as 'backwards into the future'. Such a strict approach fails to do full justice to the rich diversity of architecture either.

Between the two dogmatic extremes of compulsive independence from history and slavish obedience to the past, there are many positions from which it is possible to search freely for new solutions without denying history. There are only a handful of architects who adopt such positions. The oeuvre of Dick van Gameren and *Revisions of Space* show that he is one of them.

Hans Ibelings

Project specifications of work by Dick van Gameren

Chapter I

I. Canalside house, Amsterdam
Design: Dick van Gameren

Commission: 1993
Client: Moes Bouwbedrijf West BV, Almere
Completion: 2000
Gross surface area apartment: 225 m^2
Contractor: Moes Bouwbedrijf West BV, Almere
Structural engineer: Heijckman Huissen
Project assistant: Marcel Driessen

II. Private house, Valeriusstraat, Amsterdam
Design: Dick van Gameren

Commission: 2001
Completion: 2002
Gross surface area: 180 m^2
Contractor: Valk Bouwbedrijf, Lisserbroek
Structural engineer: Strackee BV Bouwadviesbureau, Amsterdam
Project assistants: Peter van Assche, Helga van Wijk

III. House, Borneo Island, Amsterdam
Design: Dick van Gameren and Bjarne Mastenbroek

Commission: 1996
Completion: 1998-1999
Gross surface area: 260 m^2
Contractor: Bouwbedrijf M.J. de Nijs & Zonen BV, Warmenhuizen
Structural engineer: D3BN, Amsterdam
Project assistants: Eric Heeremans, Willmar Groenendijk

IV. Apartment at the end of Borneo Island, Amsterdam
Design block: Dick van Gameren and Bjarne Mastenbroek
Design apartment: Dick van Gameren

Commission: 1993
Client block: Smit's Bouwbedrijf BV, Beverwijk
Completion: 1999

Gross surface area: 120 m^2
Contractor: Smit's Bouwbedrijf BV, Beverwijk
Structural engineer: Smit's Bouwbedrijf BV, Beverwijk
Project assistants: Willmar Groenendijk, Jacco van de Linden, Leo de Winter

V. Apartment beside the Singel, Amsterdam
Design: Dick van Gameren

Commission: 2001
Completion: 2001-2002
Gross surface area: 100 m^2
Contractor: Kluster, Purmerend
Project assistants: Mike Davis, Helga van Wijk

VI. Apartment in former sewage treatment plant, Amsterdam
Design: Dick van Gameren and Bjarne Mastenbroek

Commission: 1999
Completion: 2000
Gross surface area: 130 m^2
Contractor: Bouwbedrijf M.J. de Nijs en Zonen BV, Warmenhuizen
Structural engineer: Pieters Bouwtechniek BV, Haarlem
Project assistants: Ad Bogerman, Lada Hrsak, Paddy Tomesen, Leo de Winter

VII. Office building, Steenwijk
Design: Dick van Gameren

Commission: 1997
Client: Woonstichting De Kop, Steenwijk
Completion: 1999-2000
Gross surface area: 2200 m^2
Contractor: BAM Utiliteitsbouw BV Regio Noord, Groningen
Structural engineer: ABT, Velp
Project assistants: Willmar Groenendijk, Daniëlle Huls, Peter Schoonhagen, Leo de Winter

VIII. Dutch Embassy in Adis Abeba, Ethiopia
Design: Dick van Gameren and Bjarne Mastenbroek

Commission: 1998
Client: Ministry of Foreign Affairs, The Hague
Completion: 2002-2005
Gross surface area chancellery and apartments: 3300 m^2
Contractor: Elmi Olindo & CO. PLC., Adis Abeba
Structural engineer: Ove Arup & Partners, London
Project assistants: Lada Hrsak, Mike Davis, Matteo Fosso, Willmar Groenendijk, Jack Hoogeboom, Sebastiaan Kaal, Miguel Loos, Jeroen van Mechelen, Holger Muhrmann

IX. European Central Bank, Frankfurt am Main, Germany

Design: Dick van Gameren, Daniëlle Huls, Miguel Loos and
Bureau B+B Stedebouw en Landschapsarchitectuur BV: Freek Loos

Competition: 2003
Client: European Central Bank, Frankfurt am Main, Germany
Gross surface area: 200.000 m^2
Project assistants: Ronald Feddes, Sebastiaan Kaal, Holger Mührmann, Jan Schombara
B+B: Ulrike Centmayer, Martin Arfalk, Hendrik Dekker

X. AMOLF Institute for Atomic and Molecular Physics, Amsterdam

Design: Dick van Gameren

Commission: 2004
Client: F.O.M. Instituut AMOLF, Amsterdam
Completion: 2006
Gross surface area: 8740 m^2
Structural engineer: Aronsohn raadgevende ingenieurs BV, Rotterdam
Project assistants: Maarten de Geus, Willmar Groenendijk

Chapter 2

I. Office and apartment complex, Laakhaven, The Hague

Design: Dick van Gameren and Bjarne Mastenbroek
Elaboration and implementation: Dick van Gameren

Commission: 2000
Client: Fortis Vastgoed Ontwikkeling NV Centacon
Completion: 2002-2004
Gross surface area: 35.000 m^2 offices, 39 apartments, 1000 m^2 commercial space
Contractor: BBF Bouwbedrijf Friesland, Leeuwarden
Structural engineer: Corsmit Raadgevend Ingenieursbureau BV, Rijswijk
Project assistants: Thomas Bedaux, Javier Calvo, Ronald Feddes, Willmar Groenendijk, Lada Hrsak

II. Marktplein apartment block, Emmen

Design: Dick van Gameren

Commission: 1996
Client: Brands Bouwontwikkeling BV, Emmen
Completion: 2001-2003
Numbers: 27 apartments and 1100 m^2 commercial space
Contractor: Brands Bouwgroep BV, Emmen
Structural engineer: Ingenieurs Groep Emmen BV
Project assistants: Joep Damstra, Jacco van de Linde, Mark Sloof, Leo de Winter

III. Apartment block 23B1, IJburg, Amsterdam

Design: Dick van Gameren

Commission: 2000
Client: IJburgermaatschappij, Amsterdam
Completion: 2004-2005
Numbers: 82 apartments, 1000 m^2 commercial space and parking
Contractor: Moes Bouwbedrijf West BV, Almere
Structural engineer: Adams Bouwadviesbureau BV, Druten
Project assistants: Wouter Kuiper, Gert-Jan Machiels, Mark Sloof, Paul Vlok

IV. Residential care centre, Berkenstede, Diemen

Design: Dick van Gameren

Commission: 1999
Client: De Principaal, Amsterdam, in collaboration with Stichting Amstelhuizen, Amsterdam
Completion: 2005-2006
Gross surface area: 21.820 m^2
Contractor: Heijmerink Bouw Utrecht BV, Bunnik
Structural engineer: Zonneveld BV Ingenieursbureau, Rotterdam
Project assistants: Ad Bogerman, Remco van Buuren, Javier Calvo, Arjan Dubois, Willmar Groenendijk, Daniëlle Huls, Sebastiaan Kaal, Elrick Mulder, Jan Schombara, Mark Sloof, Bastiaan Vlierboom, Helga van Wijk

V. Houtrust competition, The Hague

Design: Dick van Gameren with Miguel Loos

Competition: 2003
Client: A.M. Wonen, Thunissen Ontwikkeling BV
Gross surface area: 20.000 m^2 apartments, 7300 m^2 parking, 5000 m^2 school, 4500 m^2 sport
Project assistants: Maarten de Geus, Sebastiaan Kaal, Jan Schombara, Boy Schouten

VI. Zuiveringspark, Amsterdam

Design: Dick van Gameren and Bjarne Mastenbroek

Commission: 1994
Client: Smit's Bouwbedrijf BV, Beverwijk
Completion: 1996-1998
Numbers: 80 apartments, parking and park
Contractor: Smits Bouwbedrijf BV, Beverwijk
Structural engineer: Pieters Bouwtechniek BV, Haarlem
Project assistants: Arnoud Gelauff, Eric Heeremans, Titia Jansen, Gerrit de Vries, Leo de Winter, Frans Ziegler

VII. Urban study, Moerwijk, The Hague

Design: Dick van Gameren

Design: 1999
Client: Haag Wonen Woningstichting, The Hague
Project assistant: Daniëlle Huls

VIII. Housing, Huizen

Design: Dick van Gameren

Commission: 2003
Client: BPF Bouwinvest, Amsterdam
Completion: 2005-2006
Numbers: 62 apartments and parking
Contractor: Coen Hagedoorn Bouw BV, Huizen
Structural engineer: Adams Bouwadviesbureau BV, Druten
Project assistants: Remco van Buuren, Maarten de Geus, Dorieke van Steeg, Paul Vlok, Helga van Wijk, Jeroen Staats, Niels Boswinkel

Chapter III

I. Grootstal housing project, Nijmegen

Design: Dick van Gameren

Commission: 1994
Client: Katholieke woningvereniging Kolping, Nijmegen, Woningbouwvereniging Mr. C.J.A.M. ten Hagen, Nijmegen
Completion: 1995-1997
Numbers: 150 apartments
Contractor: Heijmans IBC Bouw
Structural engineer: ABT, Velp
Project assistants: Eric Heeremans, Willmar Groenendijk, Frans Ziegler

II. Oosterhout housing project, Nijmegen

Design: Dick van Gameren and Gert-Jan Hendriks

Commission: 1997
Client: Talis Woondiensten, Nijmegen
Numbers: 100 apartments
Completion: 2000-2001
Contractor: Heijmans IBC Bouw
Structural engineer: Bouwtechnisch Adviesbureau Croes BV, Nijmegen
Project assistants: Gini Corso, Bastiaan Vlierboom, Carla Wieman

III. Hedeman site urban plan, Almelo
Design: Dick van Gameren and Bjarne Mastenbroek

Commission: 1997
Client: Woningstichting St. Joseph, Almelo
Project assistants: Daniëlle Huls, Pien Linssen

IV. Singels II subsidiary plan, Ypenburg, The Hague
Design: Dick van Gameren

Commission: 1997
Client: Heijmans IBC Vastgoed, Rotterdam
Completion: 1999-2002
Numbers: 650 apartments
Contractor: Heijmans IBC Vastgoed, Rotterdam, Heijmans IBC Vastgoed,
Amersfoort Project assistants: Peter van Assche, Joep Damstra, Gini Corso, Ruben van Eijle, Willmar Groenendijk, Pieter Hoogendoorn, Robin Hurts, Sebastiaan Kaal, Thijs Meijer, Eric Meisner, Thomas van Schaick, Mark Sloof, Silvester Vermast, Helga van Wijk

Bibliography

Adachi, M., Goto, S., Hosoyamada, Y. & Matsukuma, H. (1984). *Process: Architecture 43; Kunio Maekawa: Sources of Modern Japanese Architecture.* Tokyo.

Baillie Scott, M.H. (1906). *Houses and Gardens, Arts and Crafts Interiors.* s.l.

Beaufort, R.F.P. de & Berg, H.M. van den (1968). *De Betuwe.* The Hague.

Blau, E. (1999). *The Architecture of Red Vienna 1919-1934.* Cambridge Massachusetts/ London.

Brown, R.A. (1976). *English Castles.* London.

Bucci, F. & Mulazzani M. (2002). *Luigi Moretti, Works and Writings.* New York.

Butler, A.S.G. (1950). *The Domestic Architecture of Sir Edwin Lutyens.* London.

Chaslin, F. & Höfer, C. (2004). *The Dutch Embassy in Berlin by OMA/Rem Koolhaas.* Rotterdam.

Chermayeff, S. & Alexander, C. (1963). *Community and Privacy, Towards a New Architecture of Humanism.* US.

Cherry, B. & Pevsner, N. (1998). *London 4: North, the Buildings of England.* Harmondsworth.

Curtis, W.J.R. (1994). *Denys Lasdun, Architecture, City, Landscape.* London.

Davey, P. (1995). *Arts and Crafts Architecture.* London.

Dunster, D. (1986). *Architectural Monographs 6: Edwin Lutyens.* New York.

Feenstra, G. (1920). *Tuinsteden.* Amsterdam.

Futagawa, Y. & Hara, H. (1971). *GA 4, Kevin Roche & John Dinkeloo, The Ford Foundation & The Oakland Museum.* Tokyo.

Futagawa, Y. & Pheiffer, B.B. (1991). *Frank Lloyd Wright, Selected Houses 6.* Tokyo.

Futagawa, Y. (2001). *GA Houses Special, Masterpieces 1945-1970.* Tokyo.

Garofalo, F. & Veresane, L. (2002). *Adalberto Libera.* New York.

Girouard, M. (1985). *Robert Smythson and the Elizabethan Country House.* New Haven/London.

Grube, O.W. & Seidlein, P.C. von (1973). *100 Jahre Architektur in Chicago.* Munich.

Haigh, D. (1995). *Baillie Scott, The Artistic House.* London.

Heuvel, D. van den & Risselada, M. (2004). *Alison and Peter Smithson, From the House of the Future to a House of Today.* Rotterdam.

Hoffman, H. (1967). *Urbaner Flachbau, Reihenhäuser, Atriumhäuser, Kettenhäuser.* Stuttgart.

Jencks, Ch. (1980). *Skyscrapers-Skycities.* London.

Jenkins, D. (ed) (2002). *Norman Foster, Works 1.* Munich/Berlin/London/New York.

Joedicke, J. (1982). *Das andere Bauen, Gedanken und Zeichnungen von Hugo Häring.* Stuttgart.

Jones, E. & Woodward, Ch. (1983). *A Guide to The Architecture of London.* London.

Kepes, G. (1967). *La Structure dans les Arts et dans les Sciences.* Brussels.

Kindt, O. (1961). *Einfamilien-Reihenhäuser.* Stuttgart.

Kulterman, U. (1967). *Neues Bauen in Japan.* Tübingen.

Leong, S.T. & Chung, C.J. (2001). *Alison and Peter Smithson, The Charged Void: Architecture.* New York.

Lind, O. & Lund, A. (2001). *Copenhagen Architecture Guide.* s.l.

Maxwell, R., Wilford, M. & Muirhead, T. (1994). *James Stirling, Michael Wilford and Associates, Buildings and Projects, 1975-1992.* Stuttgart.

Muthesius, H. (1905). *Das englische Haus.* Berlin.

Ørum-Nielsen, J. (1988). *Længeboligen.* Copenhagen.

Papadaki, S. (1956). *Oscar Niemeyer: Works in Progress.* New York.

Papadaki, S. (1960). *Oscar Niemeyer.* New York.

Pedersen, J. (1957). *Arkitekten Arne Jacobsen.* Copenhagen.

Powers, A. (2001). *Serge Chermayeff: Designer Architect Teacher.* London.

Reynolds, J.M. (2001). *Maekawa Kunio and the Emergence of Japanese modernist Architecture.* Berkeley/Los Angeles/London, 2001.

Richardson, M., Stevens, M.A. (1985). *John Soane Architect, Master of Space and Light.* London.

Rodiek, T. (1984). *James Stirling, Die Neue Staatsgalerie, Stuttgart.* Stuttgart.

Santuccio, S. (1994). *Luigi Moretti.* Bologna.

Spalt, J. & Czech, H. (1981). *Josef Frank 1885-1967.* Vienna.

Stamp, G. (2001). *Edwin Lutyens Country Houses, from the Archives of Country Life*. London.
Steele, J., Scott Brown, D. & Venturi, R. (1992). *Architectural Monographs 21; Venturi Scott Brown & Associates on Houses and Housing*. New York.
Stritzler-Levine, N. (ed) (1986). *Josef Frank, Architect and Designer*. New Haven/London.
Teixeira, C.M. (1999). *Under Construction: History of the Void in Belo Horizonte*. São Paulo.
Thau, C. & Vindum, K. (2001). *Arne Jacobsen*. Copenhagen.
The Architectural Review, vol. CXXII, no. 731, December 1957.
Vidotto, M. (1997). *Alison and Peter Smithson, Works and Projects*. Barcelona.
Wright, F.L. et al (1954). *Frank Lloyd Wright, The Natural House*. New York.

Illustrations

11 (1) p. 75; (2) p. 22 from: Brown, R.A. (1976). *English Castles*. London.
14 (4) p. 56; (5) pp. XIX-38 (photo: Rijksdienst voor de Monumentenzorg) from: Beaufort, R.F.P. de & Berg, H.M. van den (1968). *De Betuwe*. The Hague.
15 (1) p. 122; (2) p. 128 (photo: E. Piper) from: Girouard, M. (1985). *Robert Smythson and the Elizabethan Country House*. New Haven/London.
16-17 (1-3) pp. 48-49; (4) p. 12 (photo: NTPL /M. Williams) from: Girouard, M. (1992). *Hardwick Hall*. London.
16-17 (5-8) pp. 158-160 (photos: Country Life) from: Girouard, M. (1985). *Robert Smythson and the Elizabethan Country House*. New Haven/London.
18 (1, 2) pp. 234-235; (3) p. 236; (5) p. 238 from: Baillie Scott, M.H. (1906). *Houses and Gardens, Arts and Crafts Interiors*. s.l.
18 (4) p. 164 from: Muthesius, H. (1987). *The English House*. New York.
20 (1-3) p. 27; (5, 6) p. 28 (photos: R. La France; G. Pohl) from: Steele, J., Scott Brown, D. & Venturi, R. (1992). *Architectural Monographs 21; Venturi Scott Brown & Associates on Houses and Housing*. New York.
20 (4) p. 203 (photo: Y. Futagawa) from: Futagawa, Y. (2001). *GA Houses Special, Masterpieces 1945-1970*. Tokyo.
21 (1, 2) p. 105 from: Futagawa, Y. (2001). *GA Houses Special, Masterpieces 1945-1970*. Tokyo.
21 (3) p. 100 (photo: M. de Benedetti) from: Bucci, F. & Mulazzani M. (2002). *Luigi Moretti, Works and Writings*. New York.
21 (4) p. 94 from: Santuccio, S. (1994). *Luigi Moretti*. Bologna.
22-23 (1, 2) Plate LV; (4-10) photono: 152-153; 155-157; 159; 161 (photos: Country Life) from: Butler, A.S.G. (1989). *The Domestic Architecture of Sir Edwin Lutyens*. Suffolk.
22-23 (3) p. 140 (photo: Country Life) from: Stamp, G. (2001). *Edwin Lutyens Country Houses, from the Archives of Country Life*. London.
24 (1-3) Plate XXXIV; (5, 6) photono:79; 80 (photos: Country Life) from: Butler, A.S.G. (1989). *The Domestic Architecture of Sir Edwin Lutyens*. Suffolk.
24 (4) p. 97 (photo: Country Life) from: Dunster, D. (1986). *Architectural Monographs 6: Edwin Lutyens*. New York.
25 (1, 2) Plate XV; (4) photono: 40 (photo: Country Life) from: Butler, A.S.G. (1989). *The Domestic Architecture of Sir Edwin Lutyens*. Suffolk.
25 (3) p. 113 (photo: Country Life) from: Stamp, G. (2001). *Edwin Lutyens Country Houses, from the Archives of Country Life*. London.
28-29 (5) p. 85 from: Stritzler-Levine, N. (ed) (1986). *Josef Frank, Architect and Designer*. New Haven/ London.
28-29 (6-9) pp. 42-43 photos: Hochschule für Angewandte Kunst-Archiv) from: Spalt, J. & Czech, H. (1981). *Josef Frank 1885-1967*. Vienna.
30 (1) p. 110; (2, 3) pp. 111-112 (photos: G.E. Kidder-Smith) from: Wright, F.L. et al (1954). *Frank Lloyd Wright, The Natural House*. New York.
30 (4) p. 105 (photo: Y. Futagawa) from: Futagawa, Y. & Pheiffer, B.B. (1991). *Frank Lloyd Wright, Selected Houses 6*. Tokyo.
31 top (1, 2) p. 47 from: Joedicke, J. (1982). *Das andere Bauen, Gedanken und Zeichnungen von Hugo Häring*. Stuttgart.
31 centre (1) p. 191; (2) p. 193 from: Leong, S.T.

& Chung, C.J. (2001). *Alison and Peter Smithson, The Charged Void: Architecture.* New York.
31 bottom (3) p. 73 from: Vidotto, M. (1997). *Alison and Peter Smithson, Works and Projects.* Barcelona.
34 (1, 2) p. 322; (4) p. 332 (photo: K. Kirkwood); (5) p. 334 (photo: T. Street Porter) from: Jenkins, D. (ed) (2002). *Norman Foster, Works 1.* Munich/Berlin/London/New York.
34 (3) p. 42 from: Lambot, I. (ed) (1989). *Norman Foster : Foster Associates Buildings and Projects 1971-1978, Volume 2.* Basel/Berlin/Boston.
35 (1-3) pp. 66-67; (4) p. 68 (photo: Behr Photography); (5) p. 69 (photo: J. Donat); (6) p. 72 (photo: A. Ponis) from: Curtis, W.J.R. (1994). *Denys Lasdun, Architecture, City, Landscape.* London.
36 (1-4) pp. 18-19 from: *Architecture and Urbanism*, No. 401 (February 2004). Tokyo.
68-69 (1, 2) p. 378; (3, 4) p. 377; (5) p. 373 (photo: C. Westwood); (6) p. 375 (photo: C. Westwood); (7). p. 383; (8) p. 374 from: *The Architectural Review*, vol. CXXII, nr. 731 (December 1957). Westminster.
70-71 (1, 2, 3) p. 52 from: Adachi, M., Goto, S., Hosoyamada, Y. & Matsukuma, H. (1984). *Process: Architecture 43; Kunio Maekawa: Sources of Modern Japanese Architecture.* Tokyo.
70-71 (4) (photo: W. Yoshio) from: Suzuki, H. & Banham, R. (1985). *Contemporary Architecture of Japan, 1958-1984.* New York.
70-71 (5) p. 136 (photo: Y. Watanabe) from: Joedicke, J. (1969). *Architecture since 1945, Sources and Directions.* London.
70-71 (6, 7) pp. 192; 193 (photos: W. Yoshio) from: Reynolds, J.M. (2001). *Maekawa Kunio and the Emergence of Japanese modernist Architecture.* Berkeley/Los Angeles/London, 2001.
72-73 (1, 3; 4) p. 112 from: Schneider, F. (ed) (1994). *Grundrissatlas, Wohnungsbau.* Basel/Berlin/Boston.
72-73 (2) p. 152; (5) p. 157 (photo: Chicago Aerial Surrey) from: Grube, O.W. & Seidlein, P.C. von (1973). *100 Jahre Architektur in Chicago.* Munich.
72-73 (6) p. 34 (photo: A. Boyarsky/The Architectural Association) from: Jencks, Ch. (1980). *Skyscrapers-Skycities.* London.
74-75 (1, 2) pp. 42-43; (3, 4) p. 12-13 (photos: Y. Futagawa) from: Futagawa, Y. & Hara, H. (1971). *GA 4, Kevin Roche & John Dinkeloo, The Ford Foundation & The Oakland Museum.* Tokyo.
76-77 (1) p. 11 from: Rodiek, T. (1984). *James Stirling, Die Neue Staatsgalerie, Stuttgart.* Stuttgart.
76-77 (2, 5) p. 62 (photos: R. Bryant); (3) p. 58 (photo: A. Hunter); (4) p. 62 (photo: P. Walser) from: Maxwell, R., Wilford, M. & Muirhead, T. (1994). *James Stirling, Michael Wilford and Associates, Buildings and Projects, 1975-1992.* Stuttgart.
78-79 (1, 2, 3) pp. 251-252; (5) p. 257; (6) p. 249 (photo: M. Carapetian); (7) p. 265 (foto H. Snoek); (8) pp. 268-269) (photo: M. Carapetian) from: Leong, S.T. & Chung, C.J. (2001). *Alison and Peter Smithson, The Charged Void: Architecture.* New York.
78-79 (4) p. 115 from: Kepes, G. (1967). *La Structure dans les Arts et dans les Sciences.* Brussels.
81 (2, 3) p. 87 from: Santuccio, S. (1994). *Luigi Moretti.* Bologna.
81 (4) p. 94; (5) p. 98 (photos: M. De Benedetti) from: Bucci, F. & Mulazzani M. (2002). *Luigi Moretti, Works and Writings.* New York.
83 (1) p. 213; (2) p. 250; (3) p. 222 (G. Sampson; R. Taylor); (4) p. 235 (J. M. Gandy); (5) p. 209 (photo: G. Butler) from: Richardson, M., Stevens, M.A. (1985). *John Soane-Architect, Master of Space and Light.* London.
84 (1) p. 296; (2) p. 297; (3) p. 366 (photos: Wiener Stadt- und Landesarchiv) from: Blau, E. (1999). *The Architecture of Red Vienna 1919-1934.* Cambridge Massachusetts/ London.
85 (4) p. 44 from: Papadaki, S. (1956). *Oscar Niemeyer: Works in Progress.* New York.
85 (5) p. 208 from: Teixeira, C.M. (1999). *Under Construction: History of the Void in Belo Horizonte.* São Paulo.
87 (1) p. 400 from: Jones, E. & Woodward, Ch. (1983). *A Guide to The Architecture of London.* London.
87 (2) p. 282 from: Cherry, B. & Pevsner, N. (1998). *London 4: North, the Buildings of England.* s.l.
108 (2) p. 114 from: Freijser V. (red) (1991). *Het*

Veranderend Stadsbeeld van Den Haag, Plannen en Processen in de Haagse Stedebouw, 1890-1990. Zwolle.
116-117 (1) p. 83; (2) p. 84 from: Feenstra, G. (1920). *Tuinsteden.* Amsterdam.
116-117 (5) p. 75 from: Castex, J., Depaule, J.Ch. & Panerai, Ph. (1984). *De Rationele Stad, Van Bouwblok Tot Wooneenheid.* Nijmegen.
116-117 (3) p. 100; (4) p. 55 from: Haigh, D. (1995). *Baillie Scott, The Artistic House.* London.
118 (1) p. 243; (3) p. 242 (photo: Københavns Bymuseum); (4) p. 245 (photo: JØN) from: Ørum-Nielsen, J. (1988). *Længeboligen.* Copenhagen.
118 (2) p. 110 from: Lind, O. & Lund, A. (2001). *Copenhagen Architecture Guide.* s.l.
120-121 (1, 6) p. 56; (3) p. 57 from: Pedersen, J. (1957). *Arkitekten Arne Jacobsen.* Copenhagen.
120-121 (5) p. 77 from: Solaguren-Beascoa de Corral, F. (1991). *Arne Jacobsen.* Rotterdam.
122-123 (1, 3, 4, 5) p. 52 from: Vidotto, M. (1997). *Alison and Peter Smithson, Works and Projects.* Barcelona.
122-123 (2) p. 75 from: Heuvel, D. van den & Risselada M. (2004). *Alison and Peter Smithson, From the House of the Future to a House of Today.* Rotterdam.
126-127 (1) p. 144; (2, 3) pp. 146-147 from: Baillie Scott, M.H. (1995). *Houses and Gardens, Arts and Crafts Interiors.* Suffolk.
128-129 (1) p. 154; (2) p. 151; (3) p. 155; (5, 6) p. 150-151 from: Garofalo, F. & Veresane, L. (2002). *Adalberto Libera.* New York.
128-129 (4, 7) pp. 38-39 (photos: O. Savio) from: Kindt, O. (1961). *Einfamilien-Reihenhäuser.* Stuttgart.
132-133 (1) p. 244; (2) p. 206; (7) pp. 166, 248-249 from: Chermayeff, S. & Alexander, C. (1966). *Community and Privacy, Towards a New Architecture of Humanism.* Harmondsworth, Middlesex.
132-133 (3) p. 147; (5) p. 148; (6) p. 149 (photos: N. McGrath) from: Hoffman, H. (1967). *Urbaner Flachbau, Reihenhäuser, Atriumhäuser, Kettenhäuser.* Stuttgart.
132-133 (4) p. 245 (photo: N. McGrath) from: Powers, A. (2001). *Serge Chermayeff: Designer Architect Teacher.* London.
134-135 (1) p. 42 from: *The Architectural Review,* vol. CXXI, nr. 720 (January 1957). Westminster.
134-135 (2) p. 135; (3) p. 136; (4) p. 134 from: Kindt, O. (1961). *Einfamilien-Reihenhäuser.* Stuttgart.
134-135 (5) p. 38 (photo: H. Snoek) from: Hoffman, H. (1967). *Urbaner Flachbau, Reihenhäuser, Atriumhäuser, Kettenhäuser.* Stuttgart.
134-135 (6) p. 149 (photo: English Heritage) from: Saint, A. (introduction) (1999). *London Suburbs.* London.

36 (5-7); **42-43** (9-12); **44-45** (6-10); **46-47** (7-11); **48-49** (2, 5); **50** (2-5); **52-53** (5-8); **54-55** (2-4); **105** (3); **106-107** (3-5); **150-151** (1-4) (photos: Ch. Richters)
37 (6-10); **56-57** (6-8); **58** (2-5); **72-73** (7, 8); **87** (3, 4, 5); **120-121** (4) (photos: D.E. van Gameren)
48-49 (3, 4); **51** (4, 5) (photos: N. Kane)
90-91 (3) (photo: Your Captain aerial photography)
90-91 (4, 5); **92-93** (2-4) (photos: R. 't Hart)
105 (2) (photo: Aviodrome aerial photography)
106-107 (1, 2) (photos: L. Kramer)
138-139 (2); **142-143** (3, 4); **147** (2) (photo: K. Tomeï)
138-139 (3, 4); **140-141** (1, 3-5) (photos: R. Klein Gotink)
142-143 (5) (photo: K. Hummel)
147 (1) (photo: M. Hofmeester)